NATASHA, PIERRE &

1812

MUSIC, LYRICS, BOOK & ORCHESTRATIONS BY

DAVE MALLOY

ADAPTED FROM *WAR AND PEACE* BY

LEO TOLSTOY

2	Prologue
20	Pierre
36	Moscow
49	No One Else
58	Dust and Ashes
72	Charming
80	The Ball
99	Letters
124	Sonya & Natasha
138	Sonya Alone
144	Balaga
157	The Abduction
172	Pierre & Andrey
176	Pierre & Natasha
185	The Great Comet of 1812

PROLOGUE

Music and Lyrics by
DAVE MALLOY
Based on *War and Peace* by Leo Tolstoy

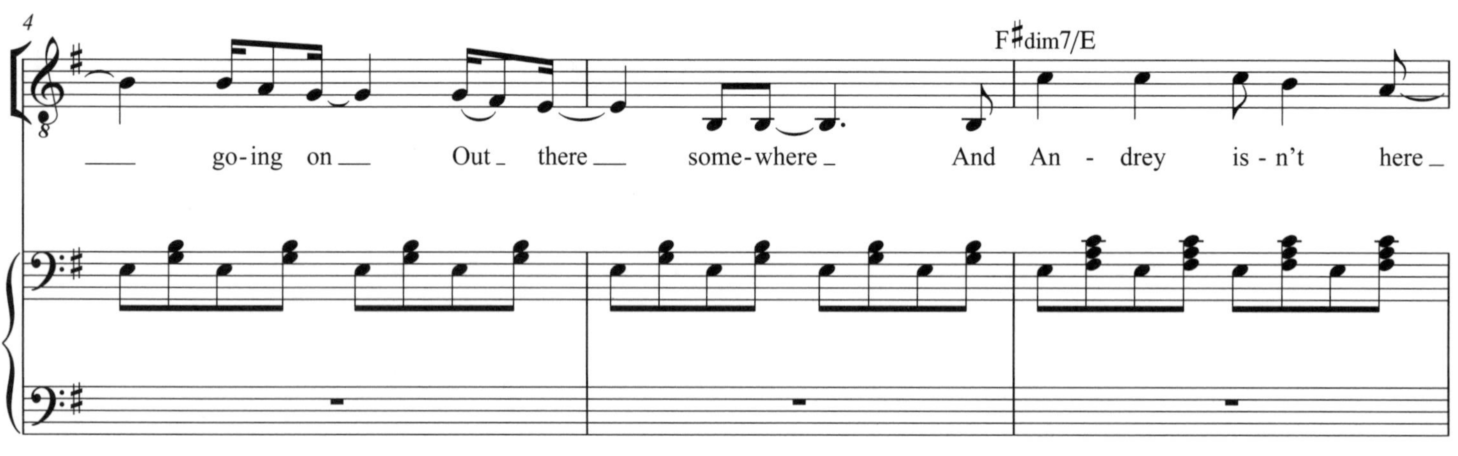

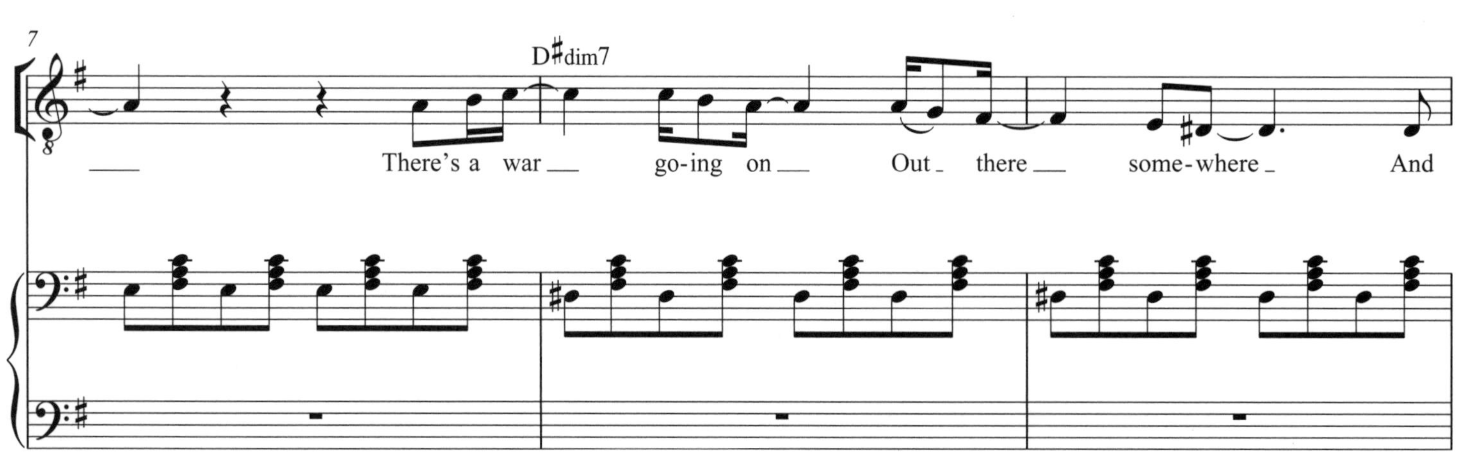

10
Em
An - drey is - n't here
There's a war
go-ing on
Out
CHORUS:
mf
There's a war
go-ing on
Out
CHORUS:
mf
There's a war
go-ing on
Out
at speed

13
F♯dim7/E
there some-where
And An - drey is - n't here
There's a war
there some-where
And An - drey is - n't here
There's a war
there some-where
And An - drey is - n't here
There's a war

19

Swing 16ths (♩ = 106)

CONDUCTOR/PIANIST:

Em

Raz dva tri!

f

And this is all in your pro - gram

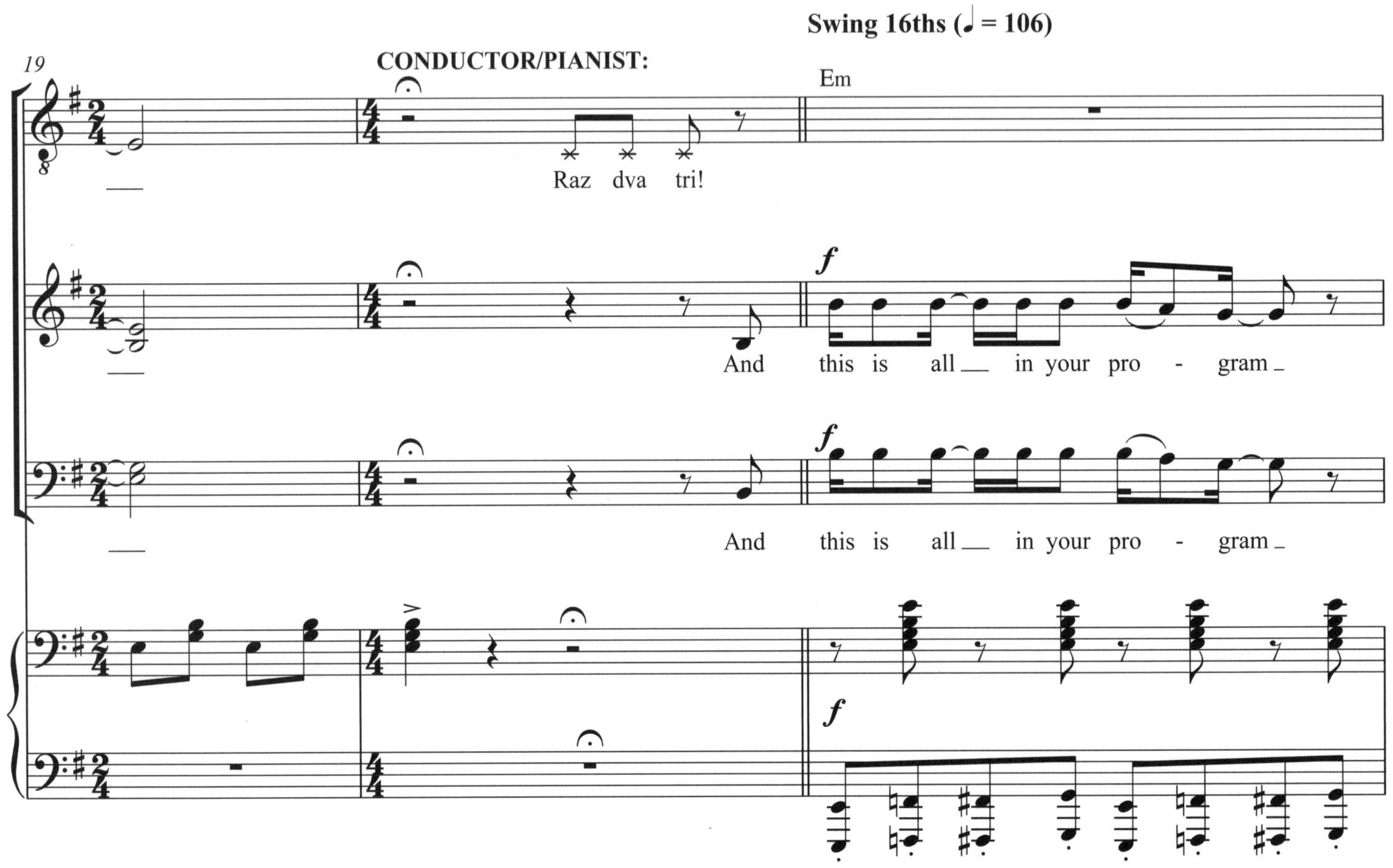

And this is all in your pro - gram

22
You are at the op - era Gon-na have to stu-dy up a lit-tle bit If you
You are at the op - era Gon-na have to stu-dy up a lit-tle bit If you
24
Adim7
wan-na keep with the plot Cuz it's a comp-li-ca-ted Rus-sian nov - el Ev-ery -
wan-na keep with the plot Cuz it's a comp-li-ca-ted Rus-sian nov - el Ev-ery -
26
A♯dim7
G/B
one's got nine dif-ferent names So look it up in your pro - gram We'd ap -
one's got nine dif-ferent names So look it up in your pro - gram We'd ap -

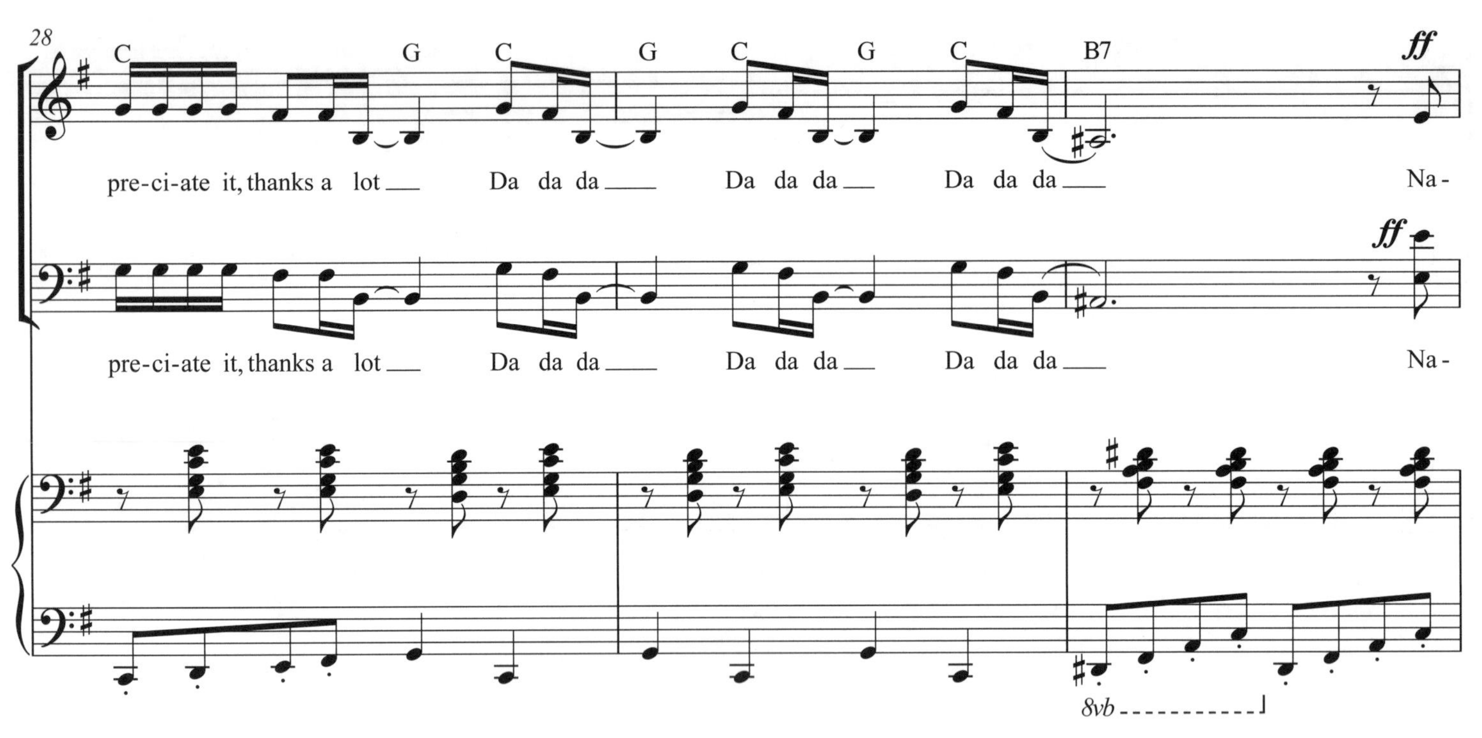

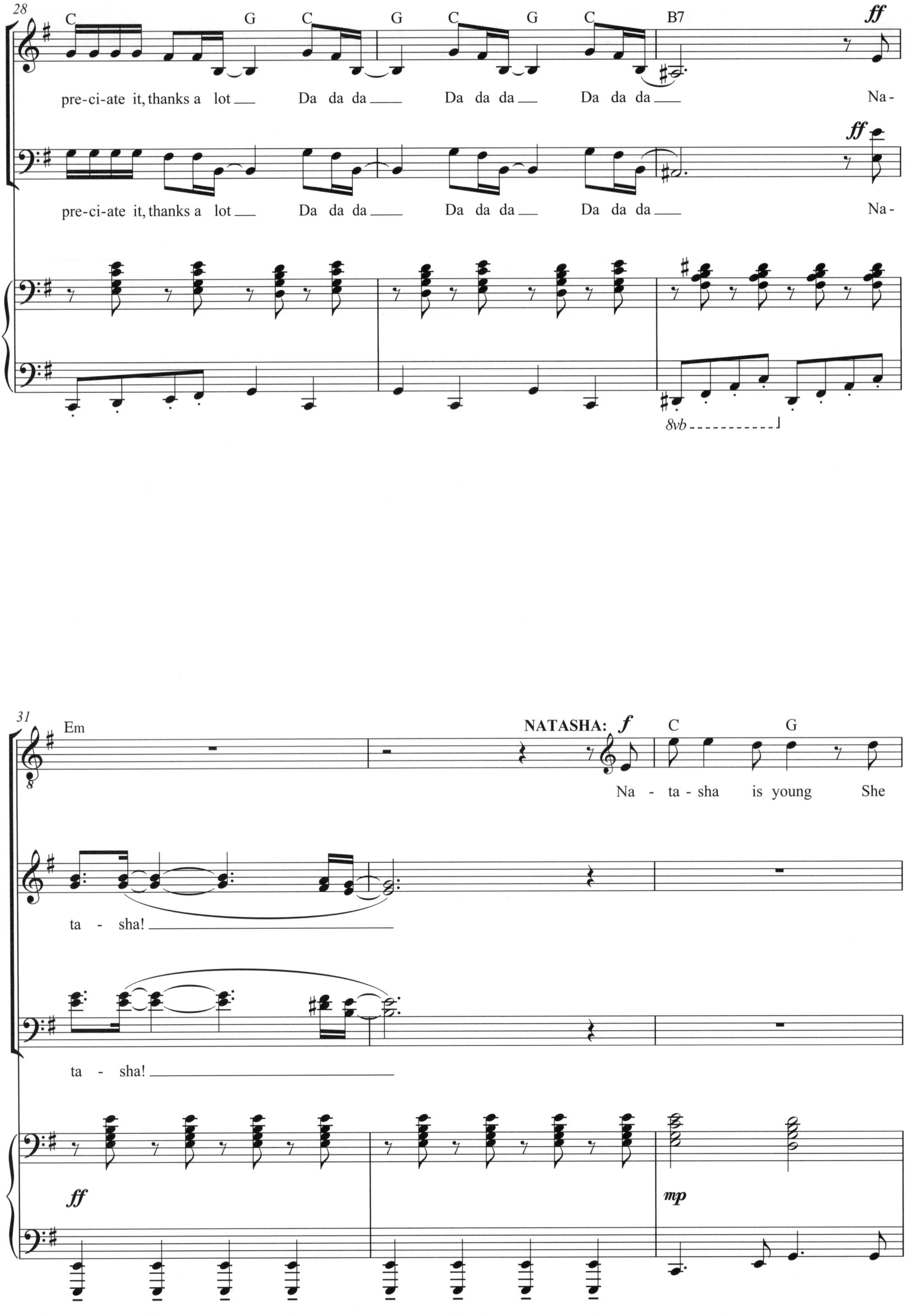

31
Em NATASHA: f C G

Na - ta - sha is young She

ta - sha!

ta - sha!

ff

mp

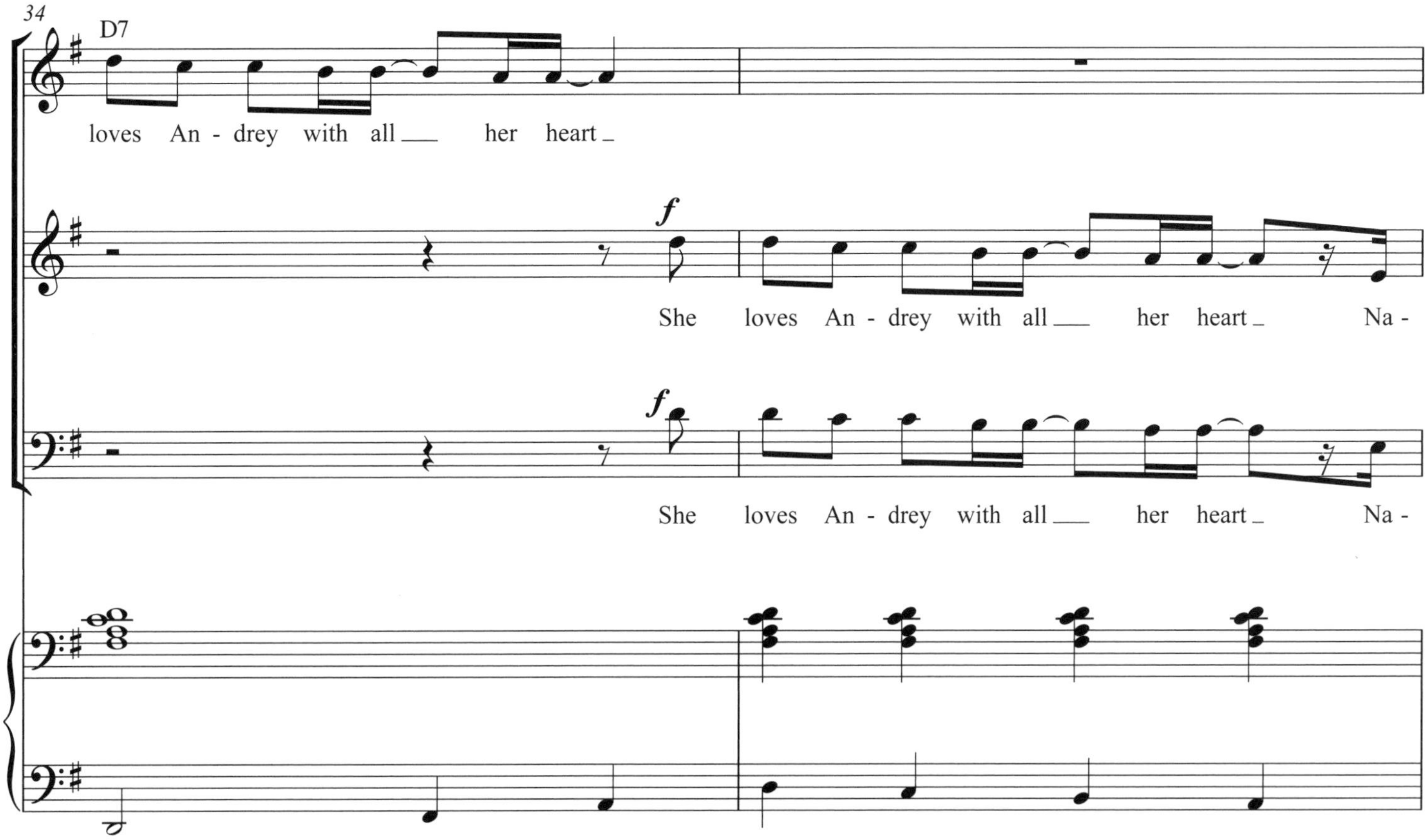

34
D7
loves An - drey with all her heart
f
She loves An - drey with all her heart Na -
f
She loves An - drey with all her heart Na -

36
Am Em B7 Em
ta - sha is young And An - drey is - n't here
ta - sha is young And An - drey is - n't here
mf

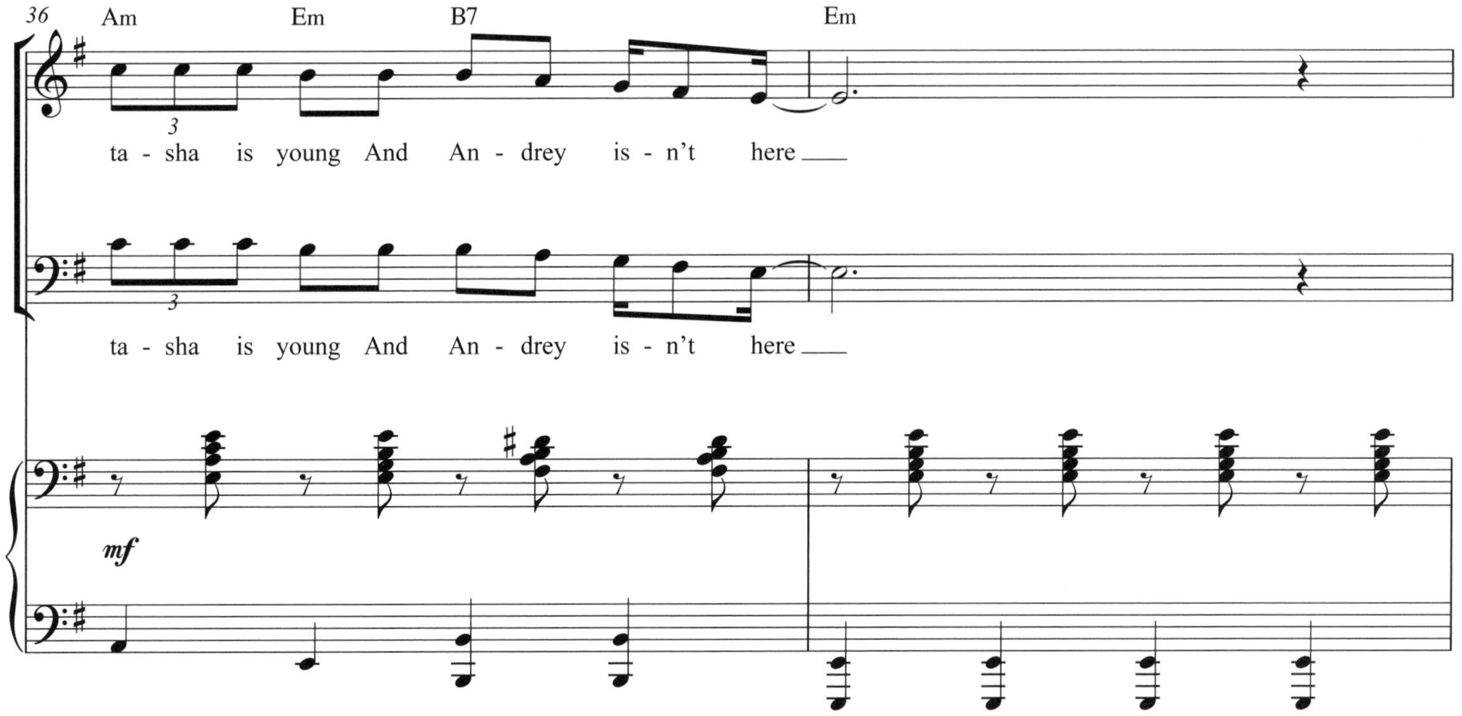

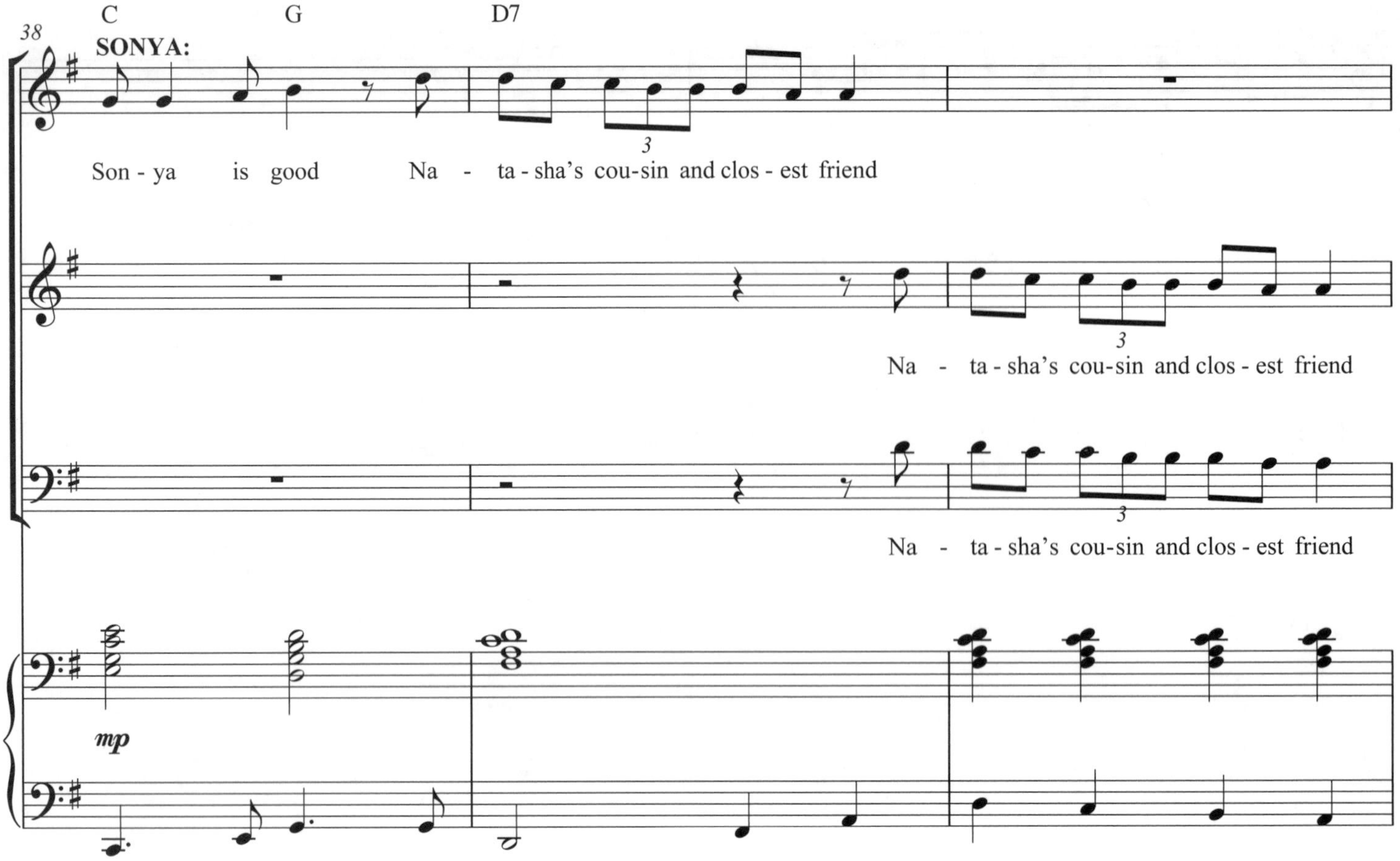

38
C G D7
SONYA:
Son - ya is good Na - ta - sha's cou-sin and clos - est friend
Na - ta - sha's cou-sin and clos - est friend
Na - ta - sha's cou-sin and clos - est friend
mp

41
Am Em Am Em B7 Em
Son-ya is good Na - ta - sha is young And An - drey is - n't here
Son-ya is good Na - ta - sha is young And An - drey is - n't here
mf

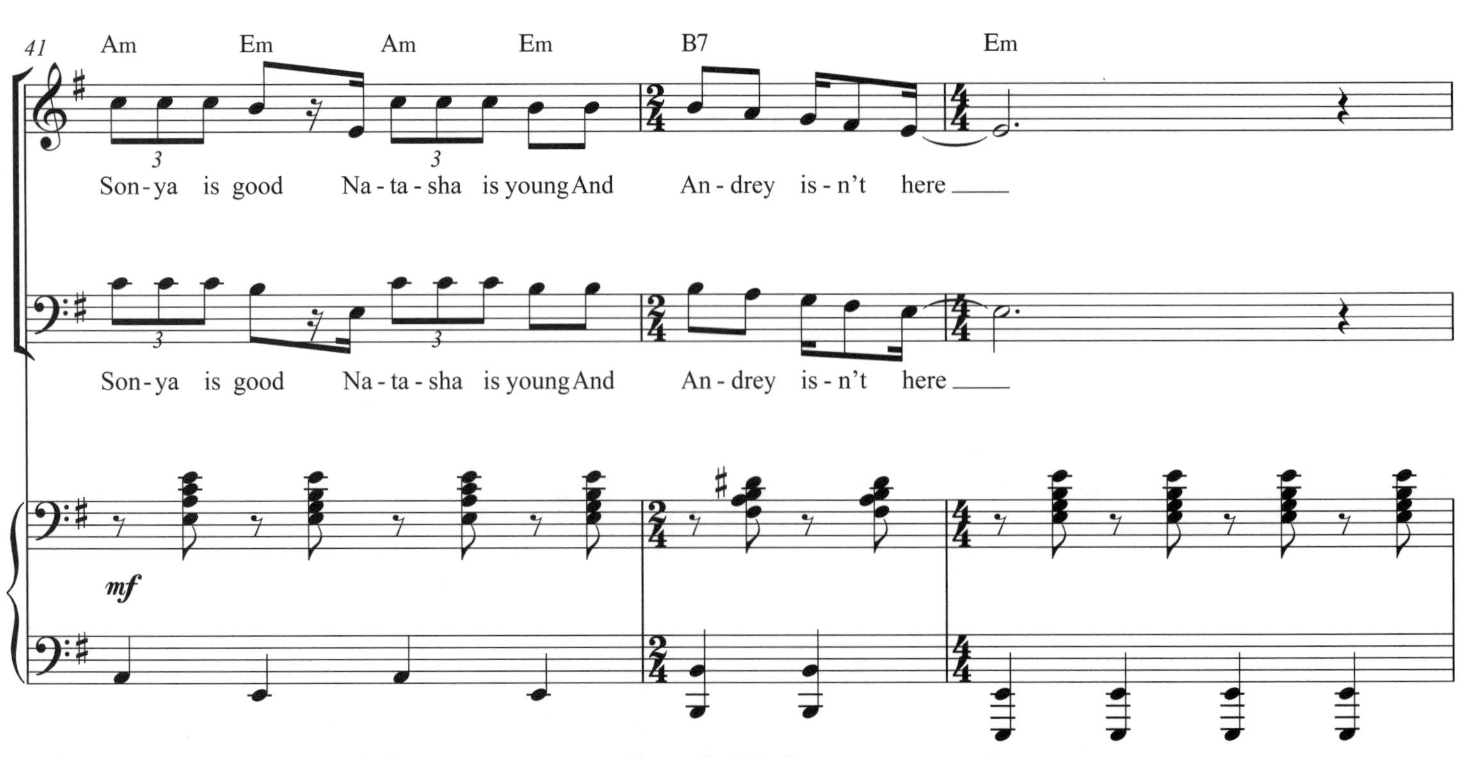

44
B7
C
G
D7
MARYA D.:
Mar - ya is old - school, a grand dame of Mos-cow Na - ta-sha's god-moth-er, strict yet kind
Na -
Na -
mp
47
Am
Em
Am
Em
ta - sha's god - moth - er, strict yet kind Mar - ya is old - school Son - ya is good Na -
ta - sha's god - moth - er, strict yet kind Mar - ya is old - school Son - ya is good Na -
3
3
mf
49
Am
Em
B7
Em
ta - sha is young And An - drey is - n't here And
ta - sha is young And An - drey is - n't here And
3

51
this is all in your pro - gram
You are at the op - era
this is all in your pro - gram
You are at the op - era
f
53
Gon-na have to stu-dy up a lit-tle bit
If you wan-na keep with the plot
Cuz it's a
Gon-na have to stu-dy up a lit-tle bit
If you wan-na keep with the plot
Cuz it's a
55
Adim7
comp-li-ca-ted Rus-sian nov - el
Ev-ery-one's got nine dif-ferent names
So
comp-li-ca-ted Rus-sian nov - el
Ev-ery-one's got nine dif-ferent names
So

57
A♯dim7
G/B
C
G
C
look it up ___ in your pro - gram We'd ap - pre - ci - ate it, thanks a lot ___ Da da da ___
look it up ___ in your pro - gram We'd ap - pre - ci - ate it, thanks a lot ___ Da da da ___

59
G
C
G
C
B7
Em
ff
___ Da da da ___ Da da da ___ An - a - tole! ___
ff
___ Da da da ___ Da da da ___ An - a - tole! ___
ff
8vb

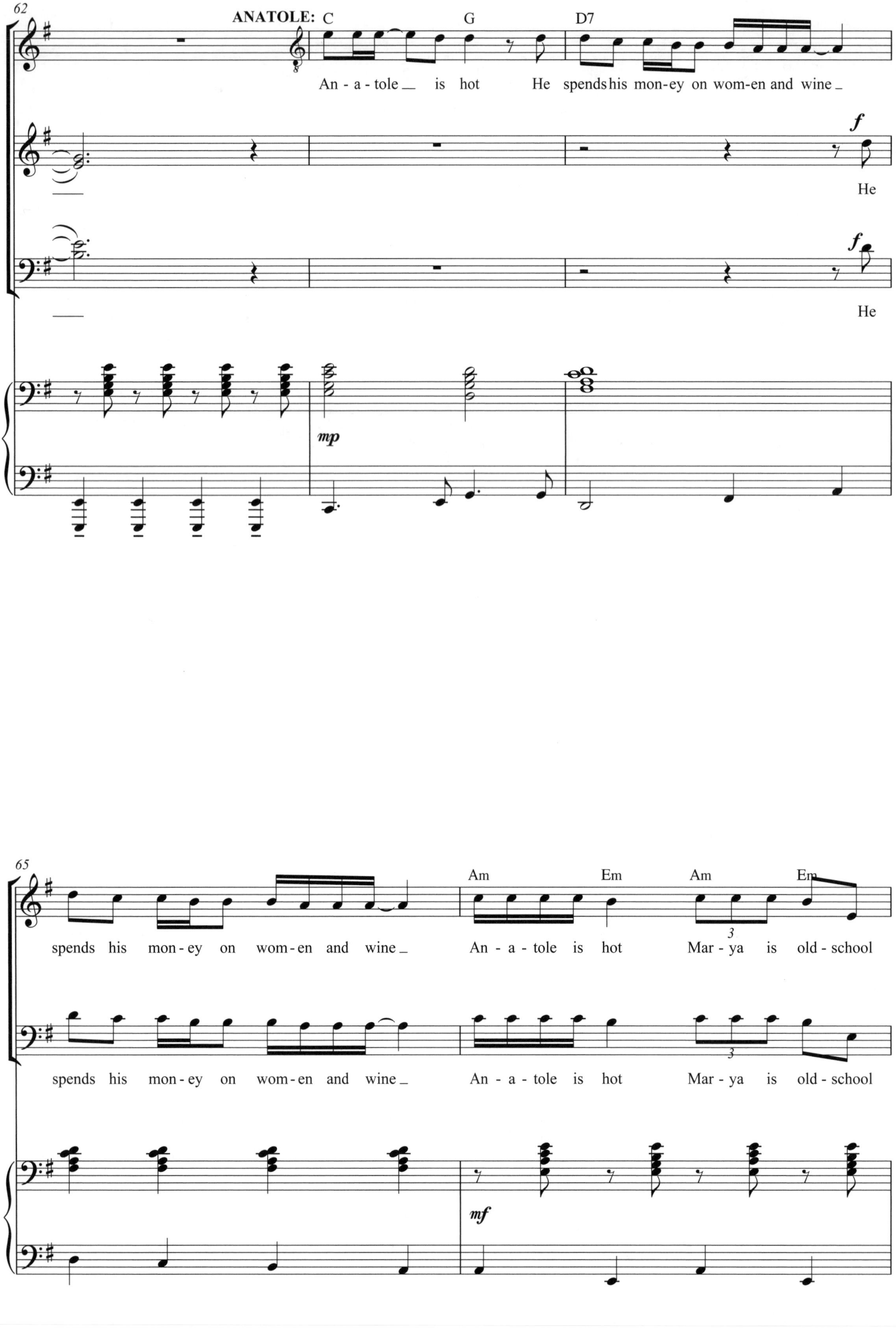

62

ANATOLE: C G D7

An - a - tole __ is hot He spends his mon - ey on wom - en and wine __

f

He

f

He

mp

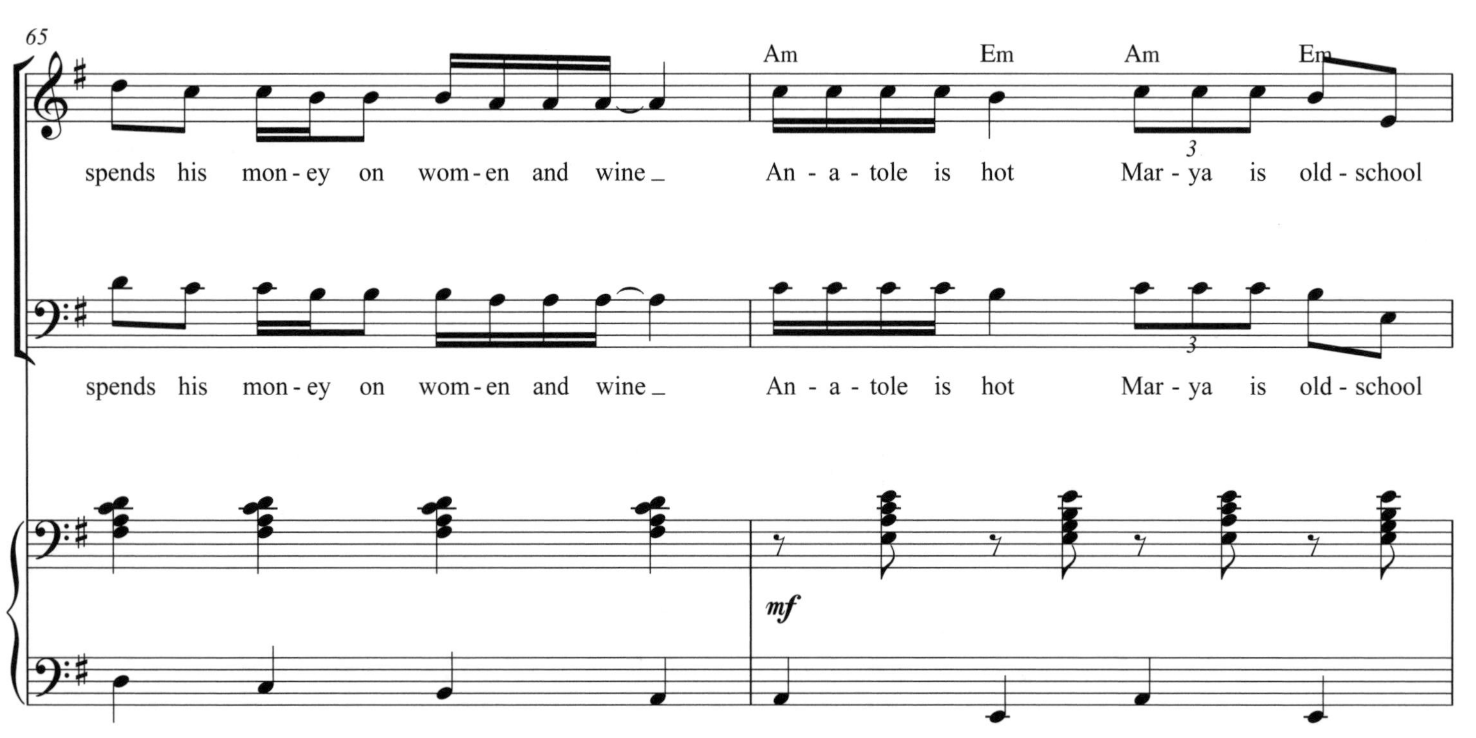

67
Am Em Am Em B7 Em
HÉLÈNE:
Hél -
Son-ya is good Na-ta-sha is young And An-drey is-n't here
Son-ya is good Na-ta-sha is young And An-drey is-n't here
70
C G D7
ène is a slut An - a-tole's sis - ter, mar - ried to Pi - erre
mp
72
Am Em Am Em
An - a-tole's sis - ter, mar - ried to Pi-erre Hél - ène is a slut An - a - tole is hot
An - a-tole's sis - ter, mar - ried to Pi-erre Hél - ène is a slut An - a - tole is hot
mf

74 Am Em Am Em Am Em B7

Mar - ya is old - school Son - ya is good Na - ta - sha is young And An - drey is - n't here

Mar - ya is old - school Son - ya is good Na - ta - sha is young And An - drey is - n't here

76 Em **DOLOKHOV:** B7 C G

Do - lo - khov is fierce, but not too im - por - tant

mp

79 D7

An - a - tole's friend, a cra - zy good shot

An - a - tole's friend, a cra - zy good shot

An - a - tole's friend, a cra - zy good shot

81
Am Em Am Em Am Em Am Em
Do - lo - khov is fierce Hél - ène is a slut An - a - tole is hot Mar - ya is old - school
Do - lo - khov is fierce Hél - ène is a slut An - a - tole is hot Mar - ya is old - school
mf
83
Am Em Am Em B7
Son - ya is good Na - ta - sha is young And An - drey is - n't here
Son - ya is good Na - ta - sha is young And An - drey is - n't here
85
Em B7
ff
Chan - de - liers and ca - vi - ar The
Chan - de - liers and ca - vi - ar The
f

87

Em

war can't touch us here — Mi - nor — char - ac - ters! —

war can't touch us here. — Mi - nor — char - ac - ters! —

ff

89

♩ = ♩. C

G

BOLKONSKY:

Old Prince Bol - kon - sky is cra - zy

MARY:

And

mf

93

B7/F♯ Em C D7

Mar - y is plain

BOTH:

An - drey's fam - ily, to - tally messed

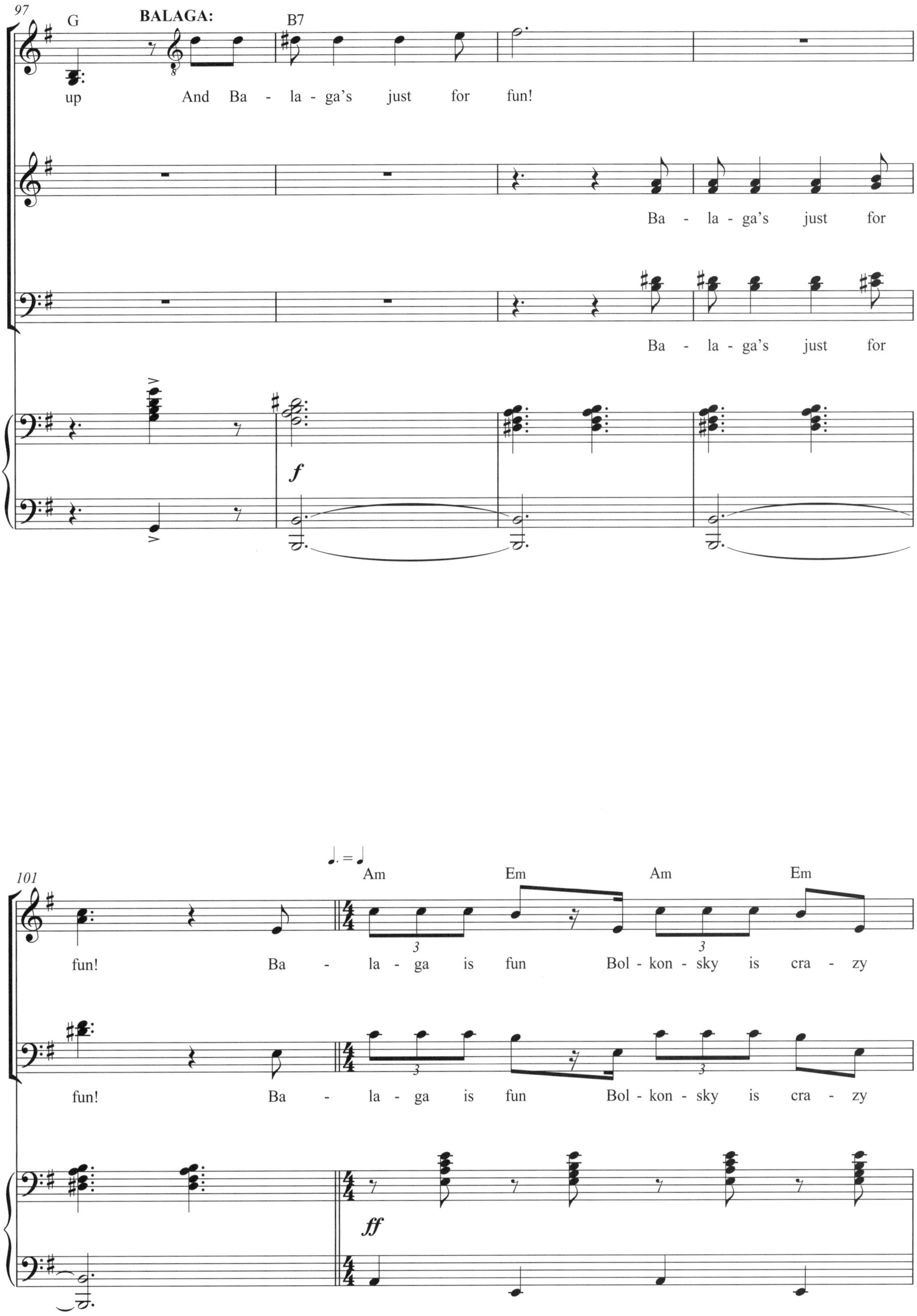

97
G
BALAGA:
B7
up And Ba - la - ga's just for fun!
Ba - la - ga's just for
Ba - la - ga's just for
f
101
Am
Em
Am
Em
fun! Ba - la - ga is fun Bol - kon - sky is cra - zy
fun! Ba - la - ga is fun Bol - kon - sky is cra - zy
ff

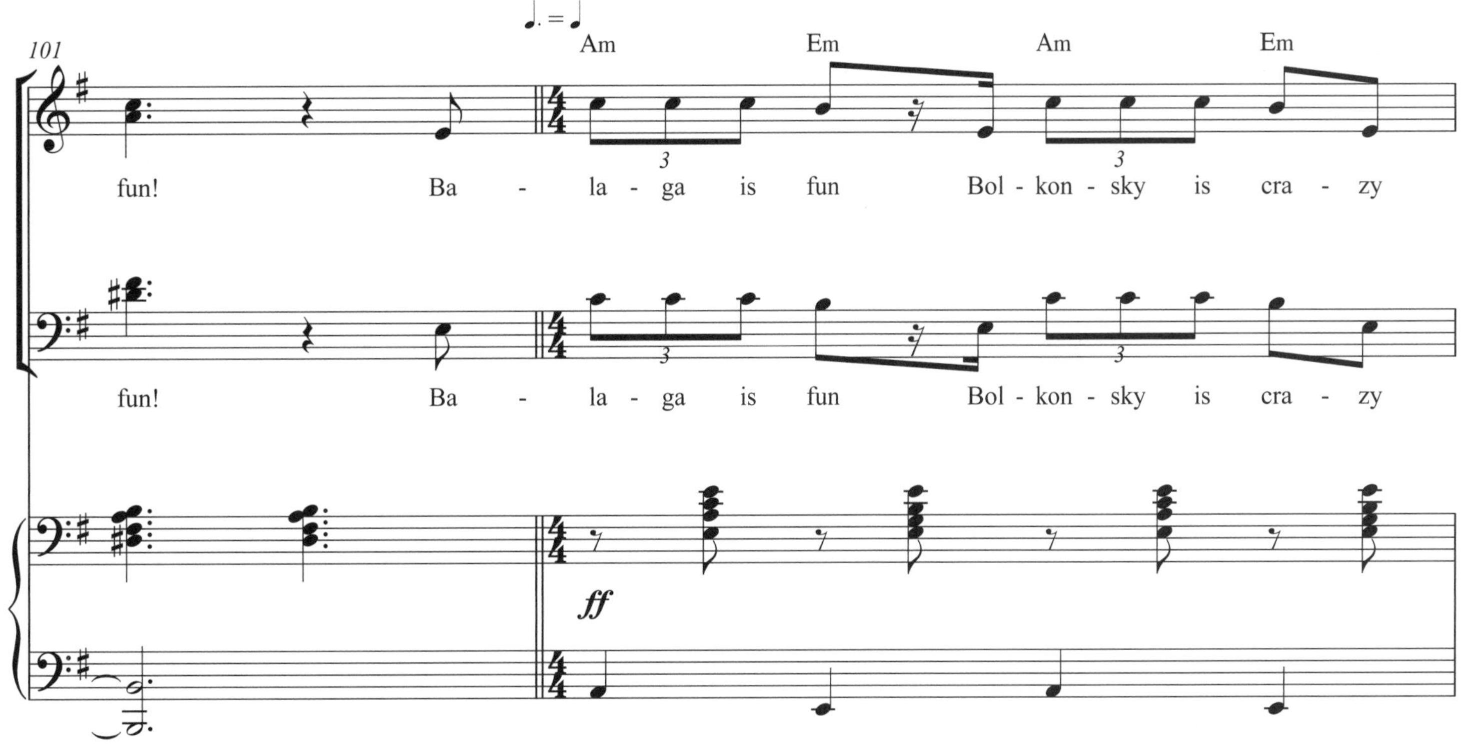

103
Am Em Am Em Am Em Am Em
Mar - y is plain Do - lo - khov is fierce Hél - ène is a slut An - a - tole is hot
Mar - y is plain Do - lo - khov is fierce Hél - ène is a slut An - a - tole is hot
105
Am Em Am Em Am Em B7
Mar - ya is old - school Son - ya is good Na - ta – sha is young And An - drey is - n't here
Mar - ya is old - school Son - ya is good Na - ta – sha is young And An - drey is - n't here
107
Em Am Em7
mf
And what a - bout Pi - erre?
mf
And what a - bout Pi - erre?
mf

109
B7♯9
Am
Em7
Dear, be - wil - dered and awk - ward Pi - erre? What a - bout Pi - erre?
Dear, be - wil - dered and awk - ward Pi - erre? What a - bout Pi - erre?
111
B7♯9
Am
Em7
Rich, un - hap - pi - ly mar - ried Pi - erre? What a - bout Pi - erre?
Rich, un - hap - pi - ly mar - ried Pi - erre? What a - bout Pi - erre?
f
113
Am
Em7
Am
A9
What a-bout Pi - erre? What a-bout Pi - erre?
What a-bout Pi - erre? What a-bout Pi - erre?
attacca

PIERRE

Music and Lyrics by
DAVE MALLOY
Based on *War and Peace* by Leo Tolstoy

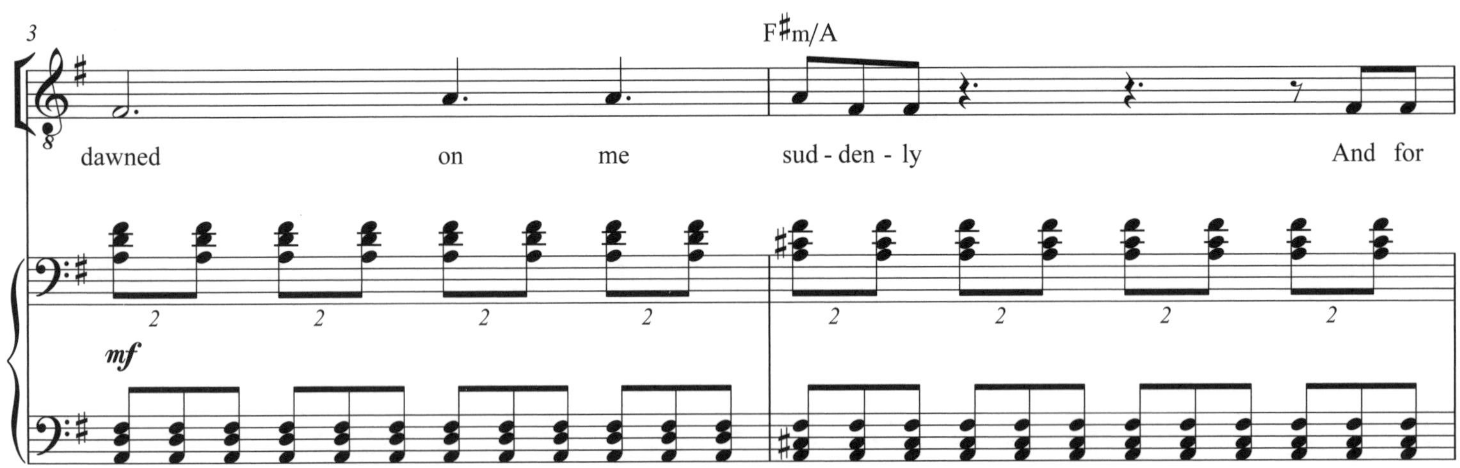

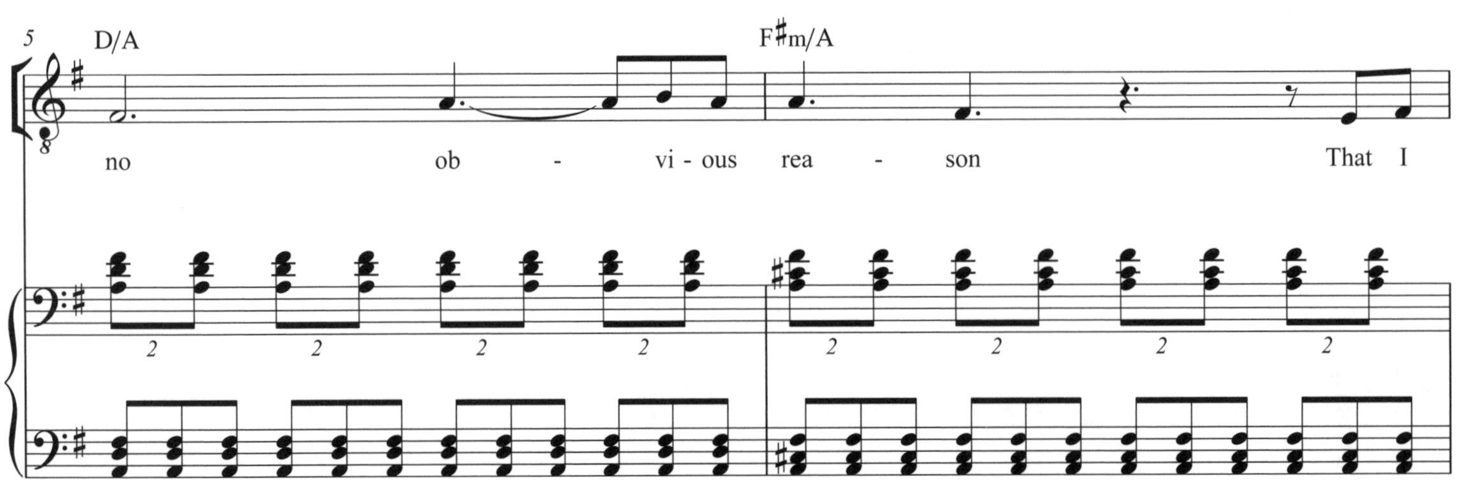

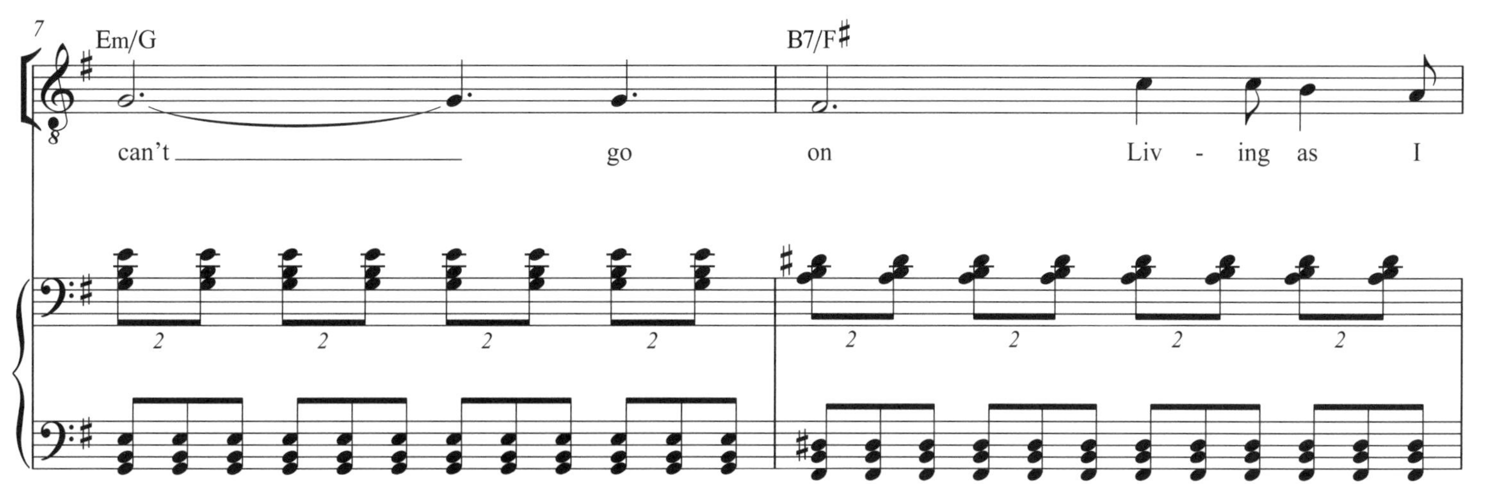
7
Em/G
B7/F♯
can't
go
on
Liv - ing as I

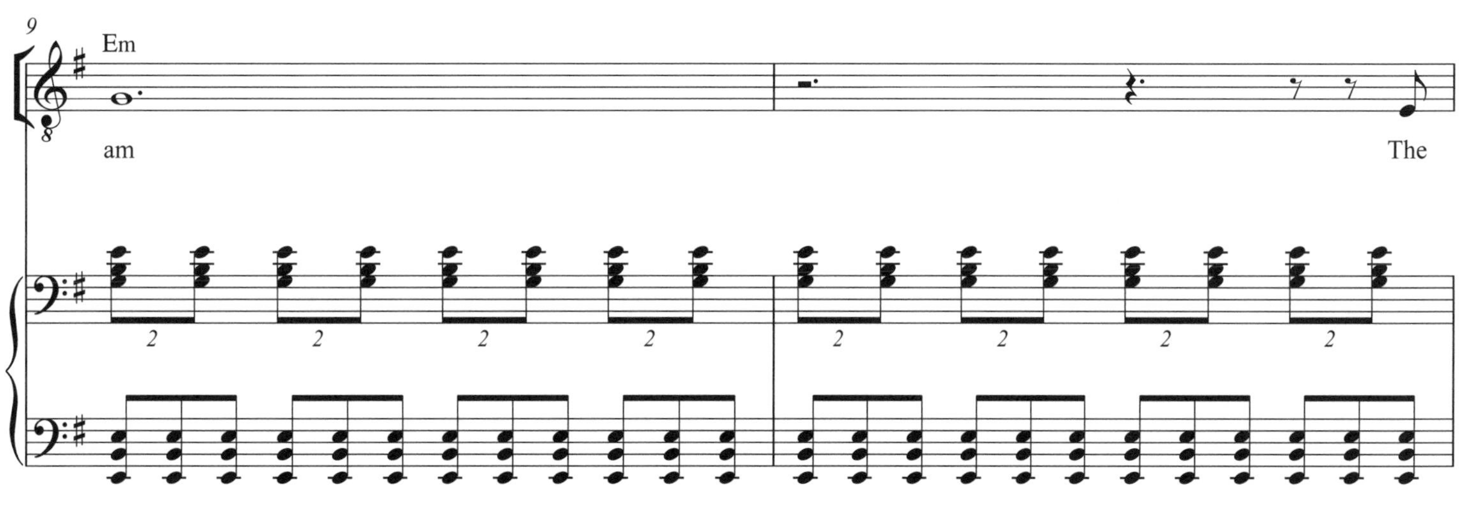
9
Em
am
The

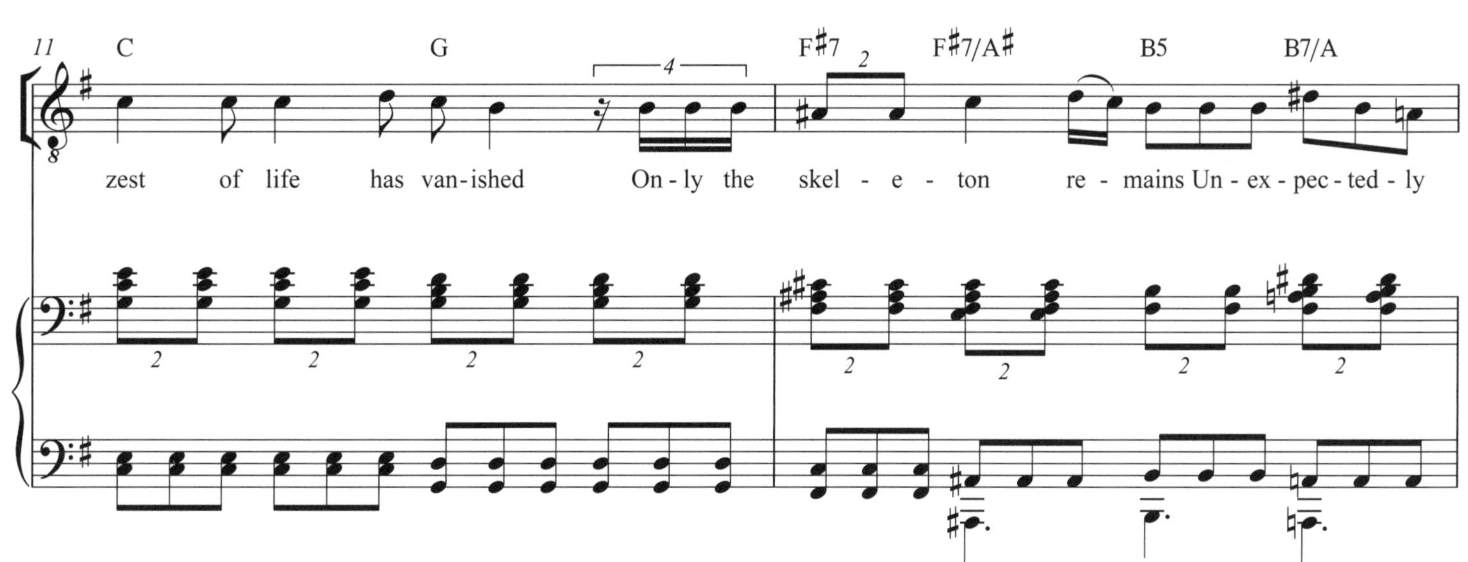
11
C
G
F♯7
F♯7/A♯
B5
B7/A
zest of life has van-ished On-ly the skel - e - ton re - mains Un - ex - pec - ted - ly

13 Em/G F#7 Fmaj7

vi - le I used to be bet - ter I used to be bet - ter I used to be

WOMEN: *p*

Ah

MEN: *p*

Ah

15 Em F#7 Fmaj7

bet - ter I used to be bet - ter I used to be bet - ter I used to be

Ah

Ah

17
Em
Em E9 Am6/E Adim7/E
bet - ter
sfp
Ah
sfp
Ah
8vb

20
Em D Am Em
ff
Oh Pi - erre! Our mer - ry feast - ing crank Our most
ff
Oh Pi - erre! Our mer - ry feast - ing crank Our most
ff

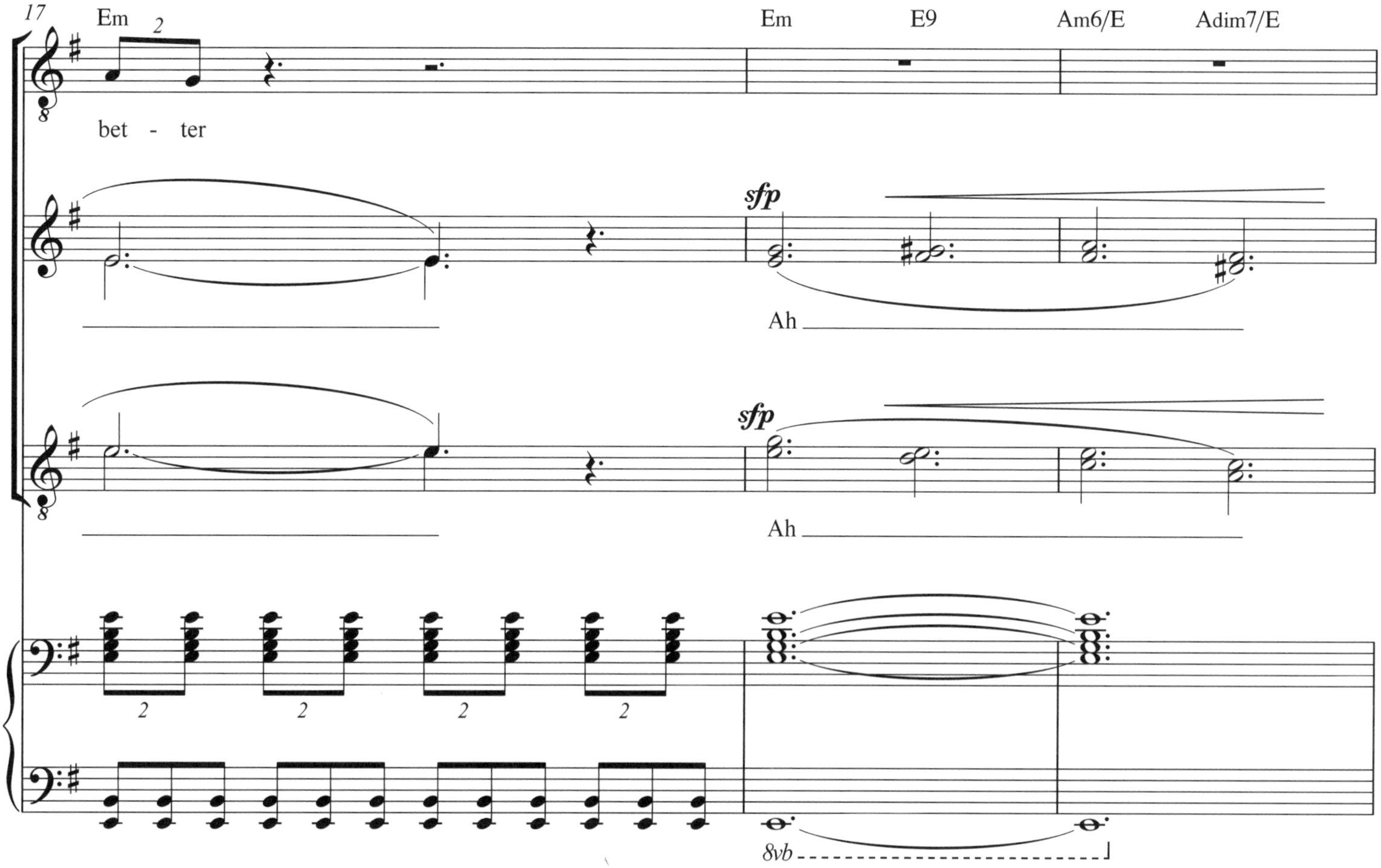

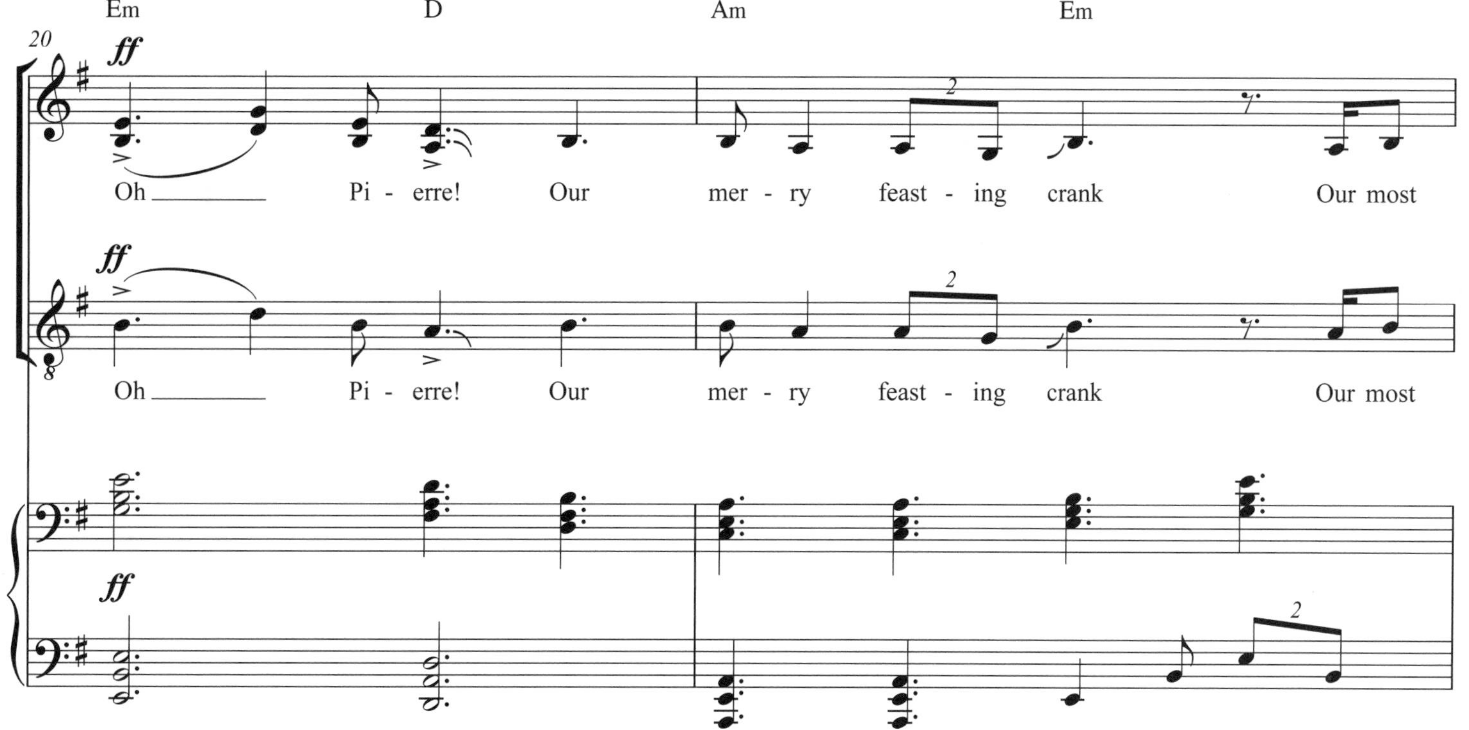

22 C/G G F♯dim7/G G | C G

dear, most kind, most smart and ec - cen - tric A warm - heart - ed Rus - sian of the old __ school His

dear, most kind, most smart and ec - cen - tric A warm - heart - ed Rus - sian of the old __ school His

24 B7♭9 Em | B7 C C/B | Am(add9)

purse is al - ways emp - ty 'Cuz it's o - pen to all Oh __ Pi - erre __ Just

purse is al - ways emp - ty 'Cuz it's o - pen to all Oh __ Pi - erre __ Just

27 Adim7 F♯dim D♯dim C | Am6 B7 Em

one of a hun - dred sad old men Liv ing out their fi - nal days in Mos - cow

one of a hun - dred sad old men Liv ing out their fi - nal days in Mos - cow

29
D/A
PIERRE:
f
I drink too
ff
f
32
F♯m
much
Right
D/A
now, my friend fights and
F♯m/A
bleeds And I sit at home and
35
Em/G
read Ho - urs at a
B7/F♯
time Ho - urs at my
37
Em
screen
An - y - thing, an - y - thing A -

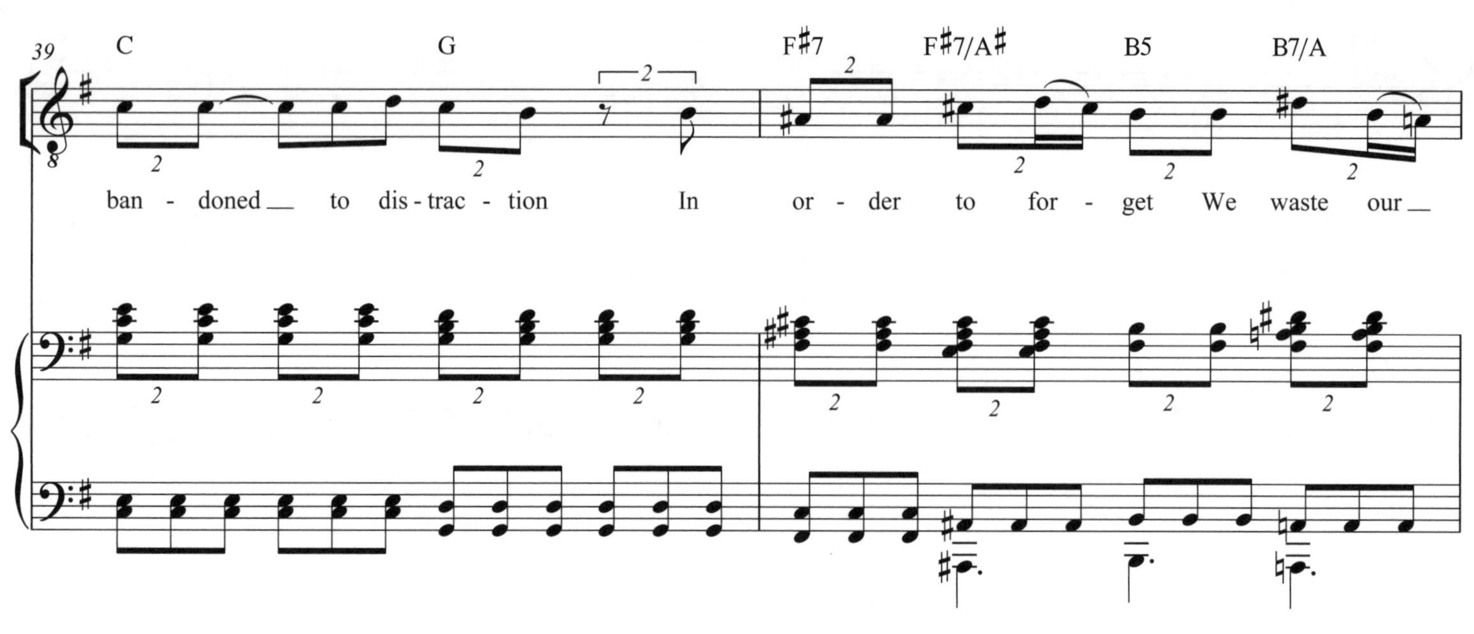

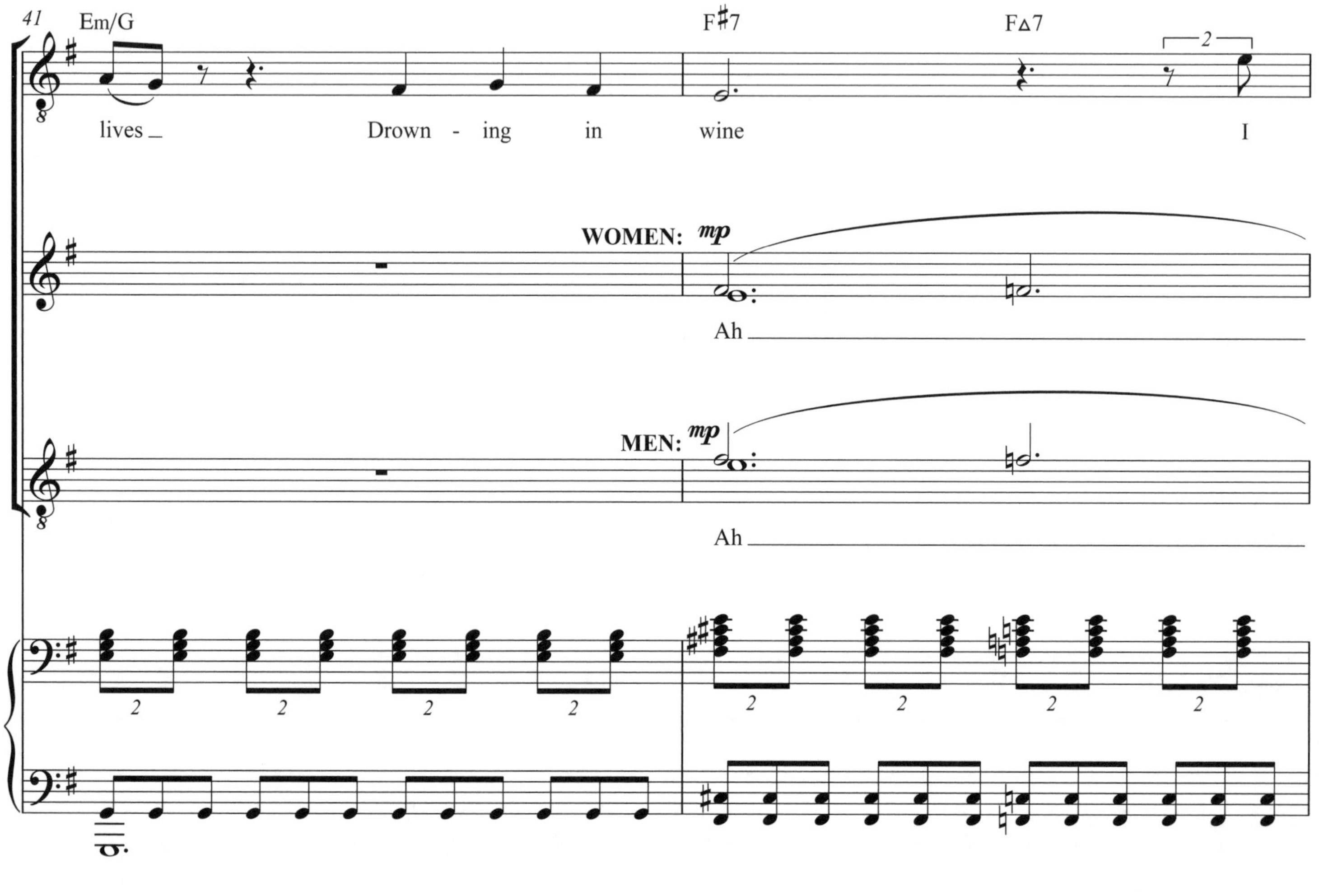

39
C
G
F♯7
F♯7/A♯
B5
B7/A
ban - doned to dis - trac - tion In or - der to for - get We waste our

41
Em/G
F♯7
FΔ7
lives Drown - ing in wine I
WOMEN: mp
Ah
MEN: mp
Ah

43
Em F#7 Fmaj7

nev - er thought_ that I'd end up like this I used to be

Ah

Ah

45
Em C G

mf

bet - ter And the wom - en they all pit - y me 'Cuz I'm

mf

8vb

47
F
E7
Am
G
F
mar - ried But not in love
Fro - zen at the cen - ter
(8vb)

A little slower (in 2)
Bm
F♯maj7
WOMEN:
50
Il est char - mant; il n'a pas de sexe; he is charm - ing; he has no

Tempo primo
Bm
B7
Em
D
Am
Em
WOMEN:
53
sex
Oh Pi - erre! Our mer - ry feast - ing crank Our most
MEN:
Oh Pi - erre! Our mer - ry feast - ing crank Our most

56
C/G G F♯dim7/G G C G
dear, most kind, most smart and ec - cen - tric A warm - heart - ed Rus - sian of the old school His
58
B7♭9 Em B7 C C/B
purse is al - ways emp - ty 'Cuz it's o - pen to all Oh Pi -
60
Am(add9) Adim7 F♯dim D♯dim C
erre Just one of a hun - dred sad old men

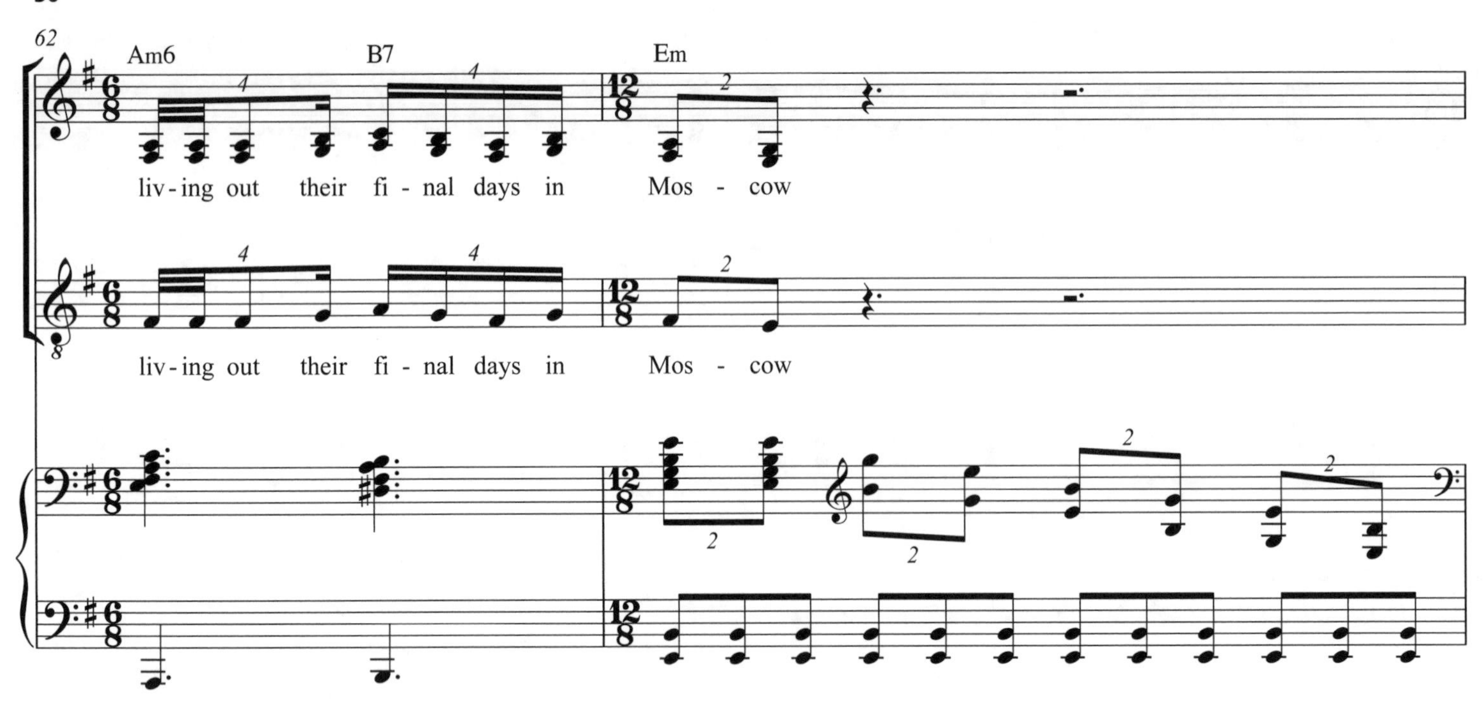
62
Am6
B7
Em
liv-ing out their fi - nal days in Mos - cow
liv-ing out their fi - nal days in Mos - cow

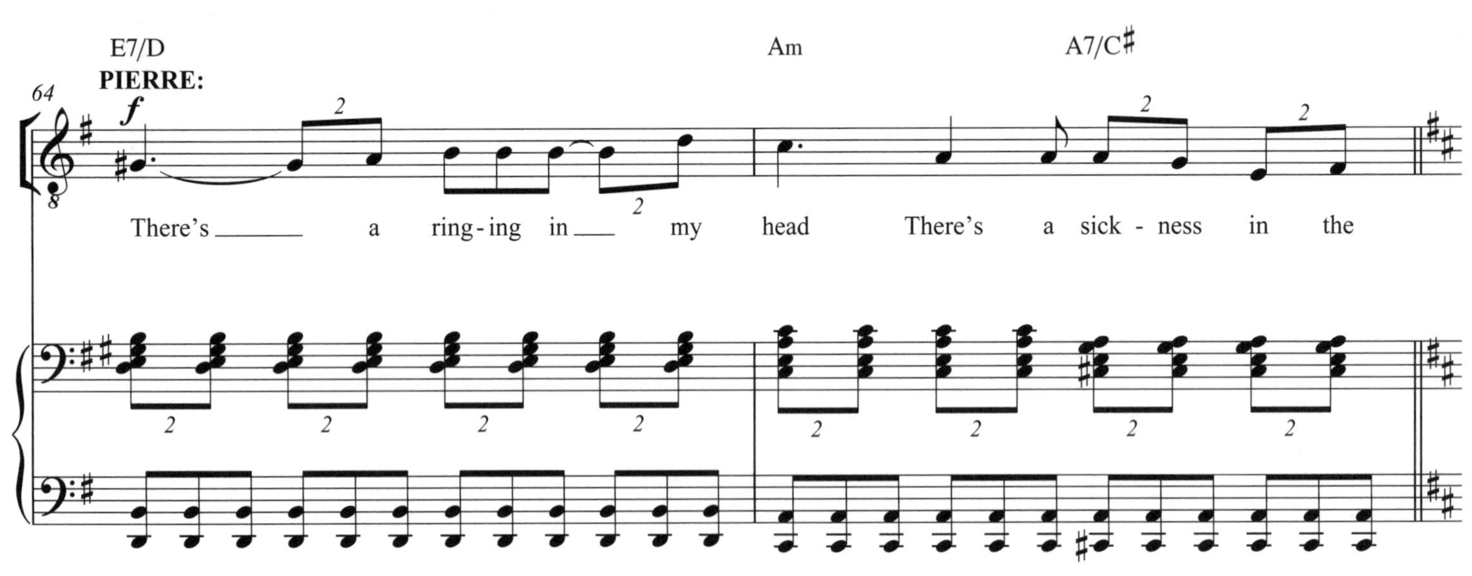
E7/D
PIERRE:
64
Am
A7/C♯
There's a ring-ing in my head There's a sick - ness in the

66
D
F♯m
D
Bm
E7
world And ev - ery - one knows But pre-tends that they don't see "Oh I'll sort it out

69
A
A/G♯
F♯m
A7
f
later" But later never comes
And how
MEN: f
And how
71
Dmaj7
A
Dm
A
many men before
Good Russian men
Be-
many men before
Good Russian men
Be-
73
G
F♯7
Bm
A
lieving in goodness and truth
Entered that
lieving in goodness and truth

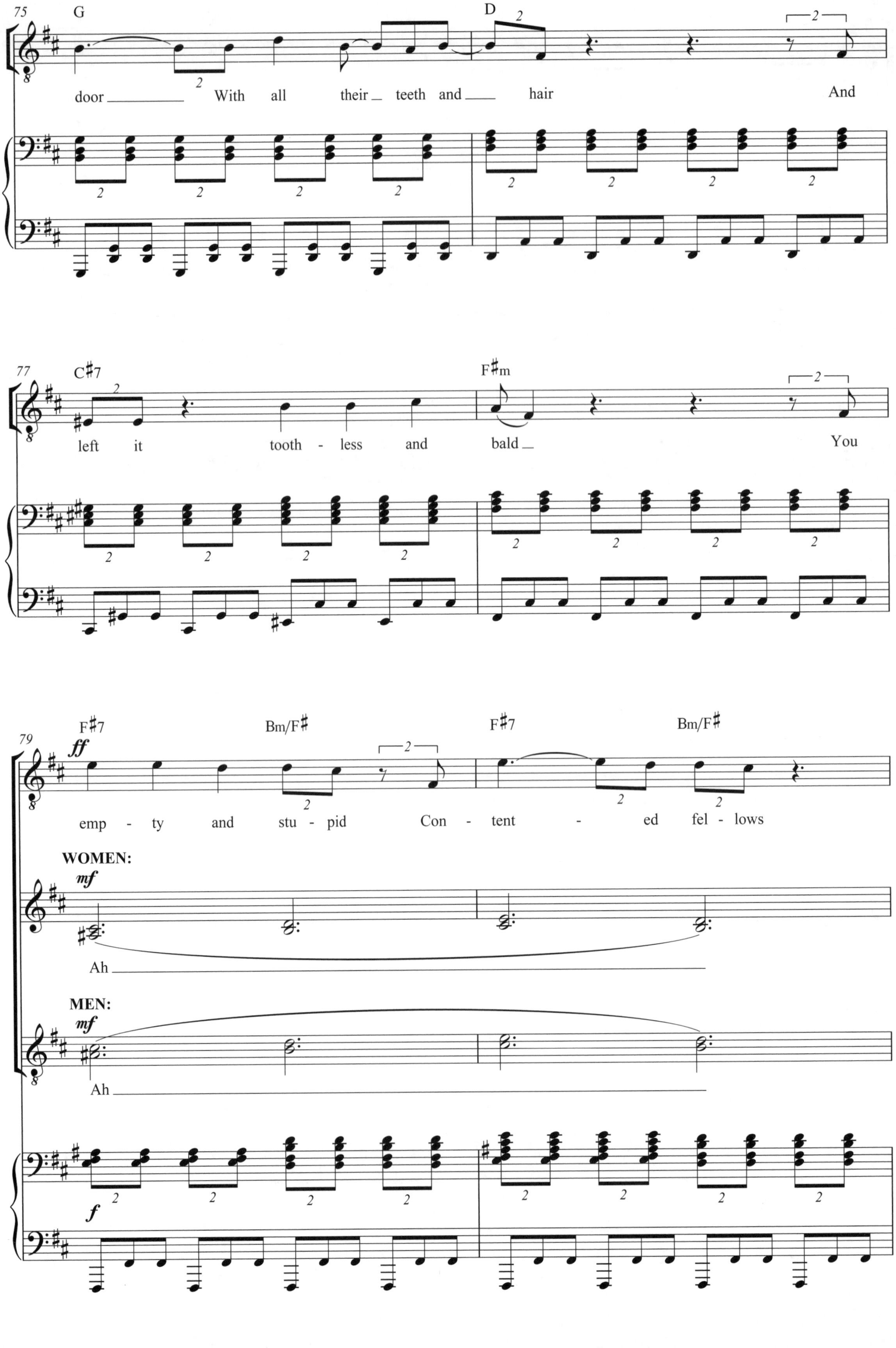

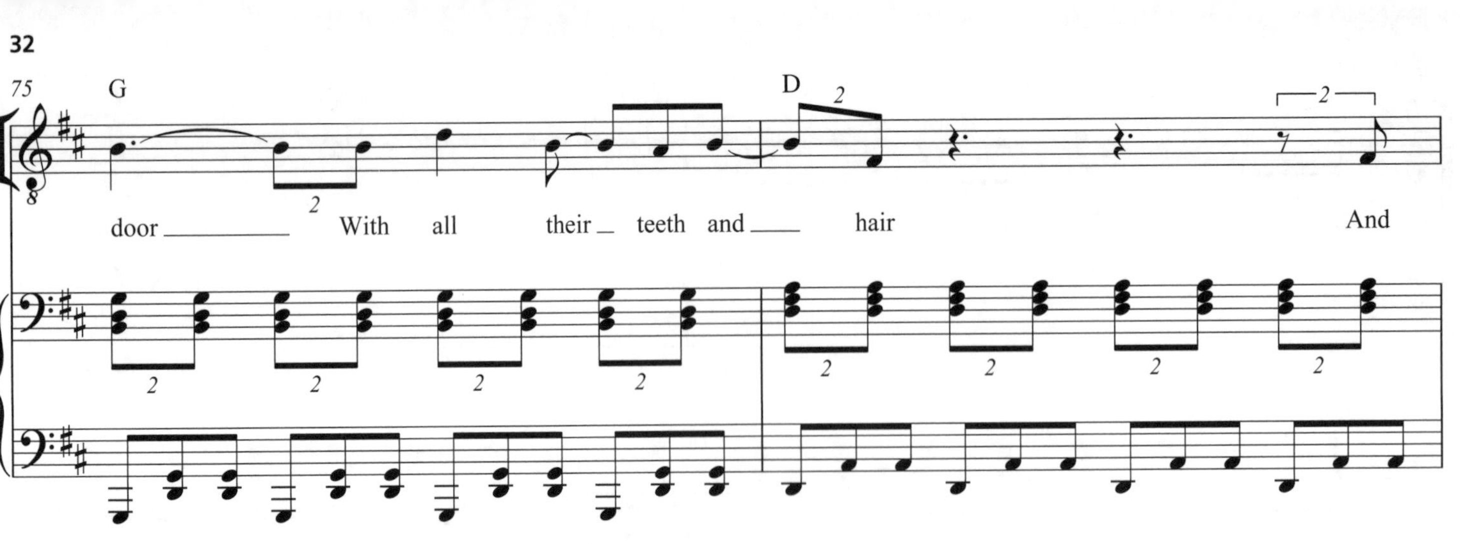

79
F♯7 Bm/F♯ F♯7 Bm/F♯

ff

emp - ty and stu - pid Con - tent - ed fel - lows

WOMEN:

mf

Ah

MEN:

mf

Ah

f

81
F♯7 Bm/F♯ F♯7 Bm/F♯
Sat - is - fied with your _ place I'm
Ah
Ah
83
F♯7 Bm/F♯ F♯7 Bm/F♯ F♯7 Bm/F♯
dif - ferent from you I'm dif - ferent from you I still want to do
f
Ah Ah
f
Ah Ah

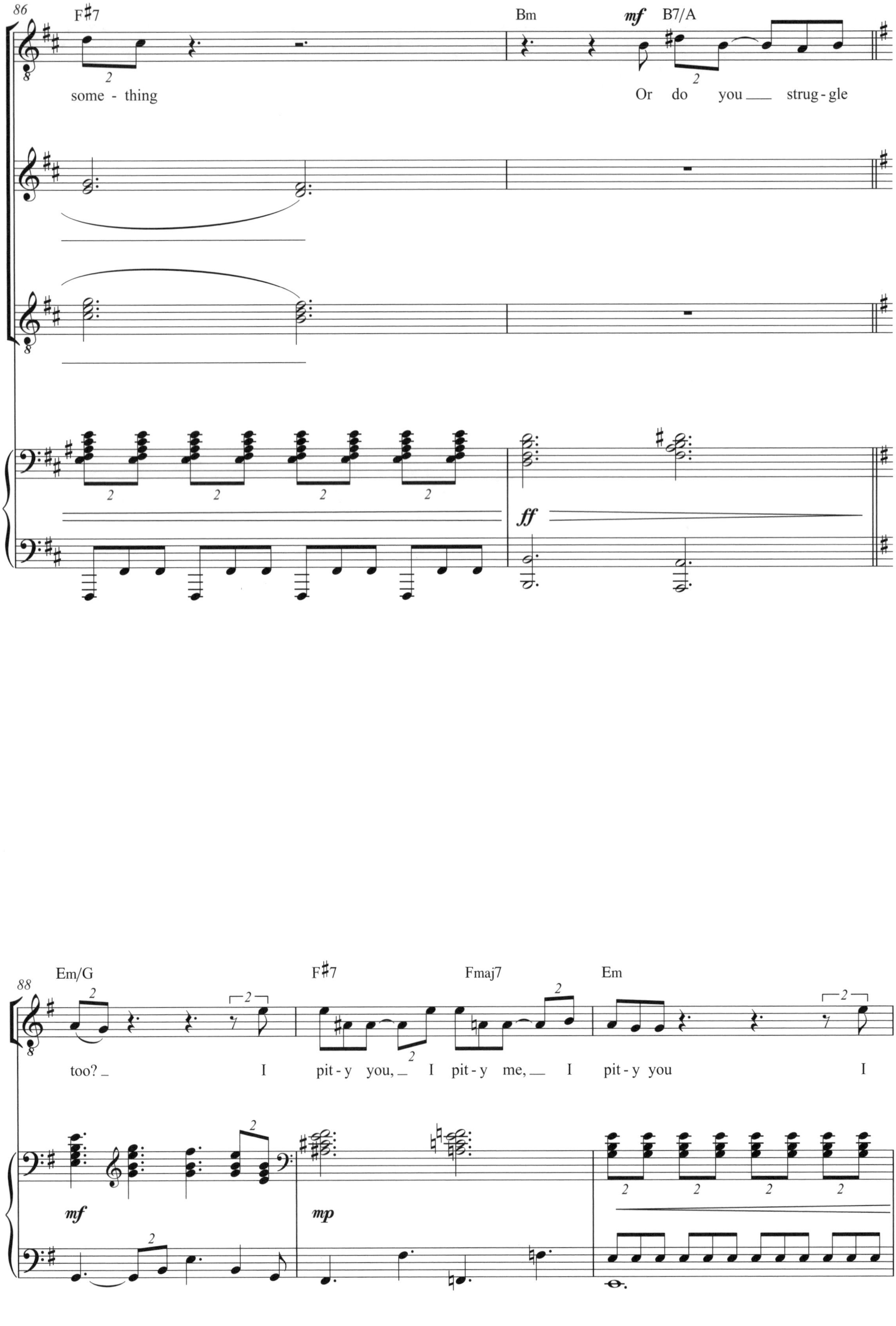

86

F♯7 Bm *mf* B7/A

some - thing Or do you strug - gle

ff

91

F♯7 Fmaj7 Em

pit - y you, I pit - y me, I pit - y you

WOMEN:

Ah

MEN:

Ah

93

ff

[Pierre cuts off]

gliss.

Ah

ff

gliss.

Ah

ff

MOSCOW

Music and Lyrics by
DAVE MALLOY
Based on *War and Peace* by Leo Tolstoy

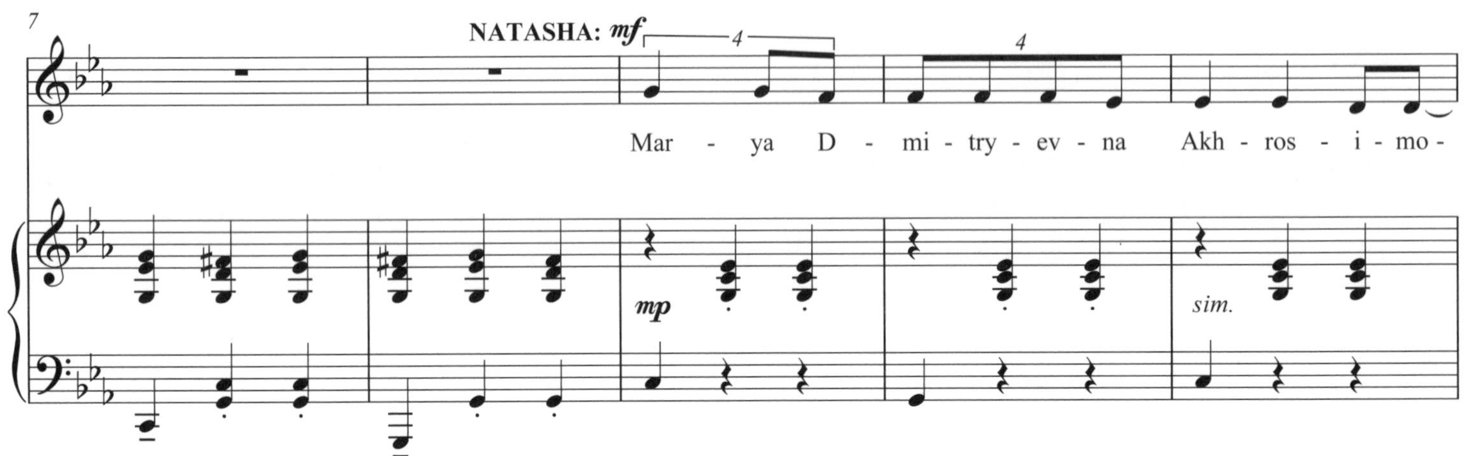

Cm
SONYA:
Mar - ya D - mi - try - ev - na Akh - ros - i - mo - va So - fi - a
MARYA D.:
Al - ex - an - drov - na Ros - tov - a You must call me
SONYA: G7
A♭ A♭/B♭ B+ E♭/B♭ B♭7
MARYA D.:
Son - ya Wel - come Wel - come to Mos-
E♭ A♭m6 Cm/G G7 Cm
- cow Where fad - ed and fad - ing prin - cess - es live I'll

41 B♭7 E♭ E♭9 A♭

take you where you must go Pet you a bit And I'll

46 E♭9 A♭ D7/F♯ Gm

scold you a bit My god - daugh - ter, my fav - orite, Na -

51 B♭7 E♭

tash - a I will touch you on the cheek

NATASHA, SONYA: *mf*

My

56 Cm

cou - sin and I Are so pleased to be with you While we

mf

61
Fm6
wait on our fi - an - cés Fight - ing in the

A little faster
66
G7
Fm6
Gm6
Fm6
MARYA D.: mf
war Bring in their things! What are you daw - dl - ing
f
sim.

71
Gm6
Fm6
Gm6
Fm6
Gm6
for Get the sam - o - var rea - dy! You're half fro - zen, I'm sure! Bring some

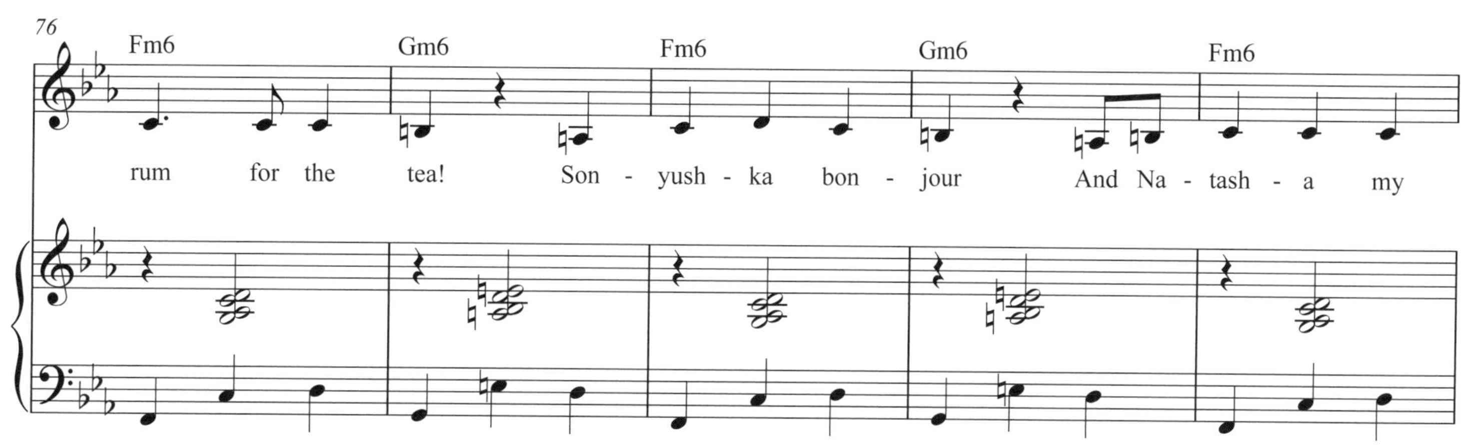
76
Fm6
Gm6
Fm6
Gm6
Fm6
rum for the tea! Son - yush - ka bon - jour And Na - tash - a my

Gm6
Fm6
Gm6
Dm
NATASHA:
f
81
dar - ling You've grown plump - er and pret - ti - er
My
86
2
cheeks are glow - ing from the cold
SONYA:
mf
91
C♯dim7
B♭dim7
Gdim7
Edim7
She said
Ga - zing at Mar - ya with
mp
96
C♯dim7
B♭dim7
Gdim7
A tempo
B+
MARYA D.:
f
kind glit - ter - ing eyes
Wel -
f

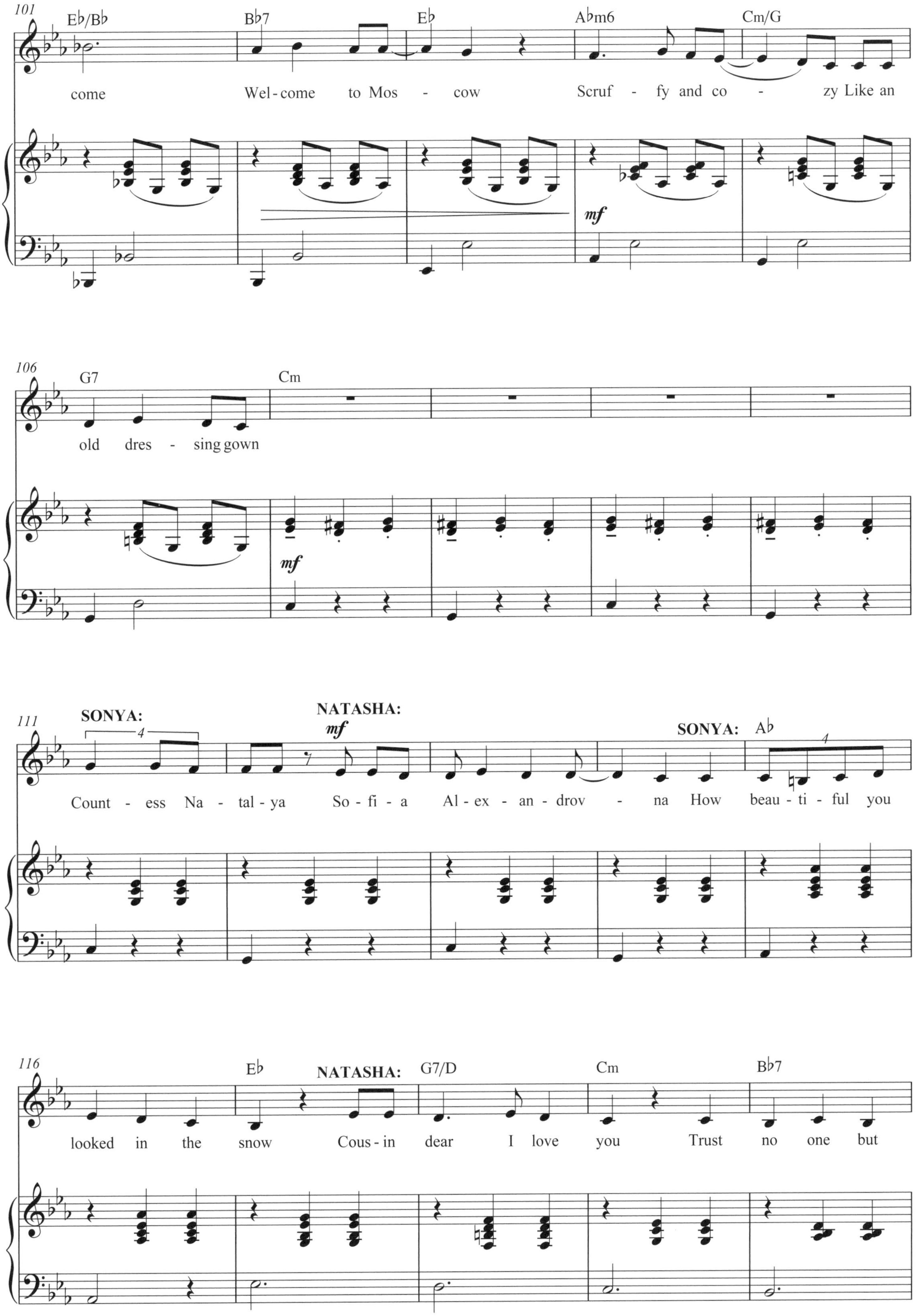

101

E♭/B♭ B♭7 E♭ A♭m6 Cm/G

come Wel-come to Mos - cow Scruf - fy and co - zy Like an

mf

106

G7 Cm

old dres - sing gown

mf

111

SONYA: 4 **NATASHA:** *mf* **SONYA:** A♭ 4

Count - ess Na - tal-ya So-fi-a Al-ex - an-drov - na How beau-ti-ful you

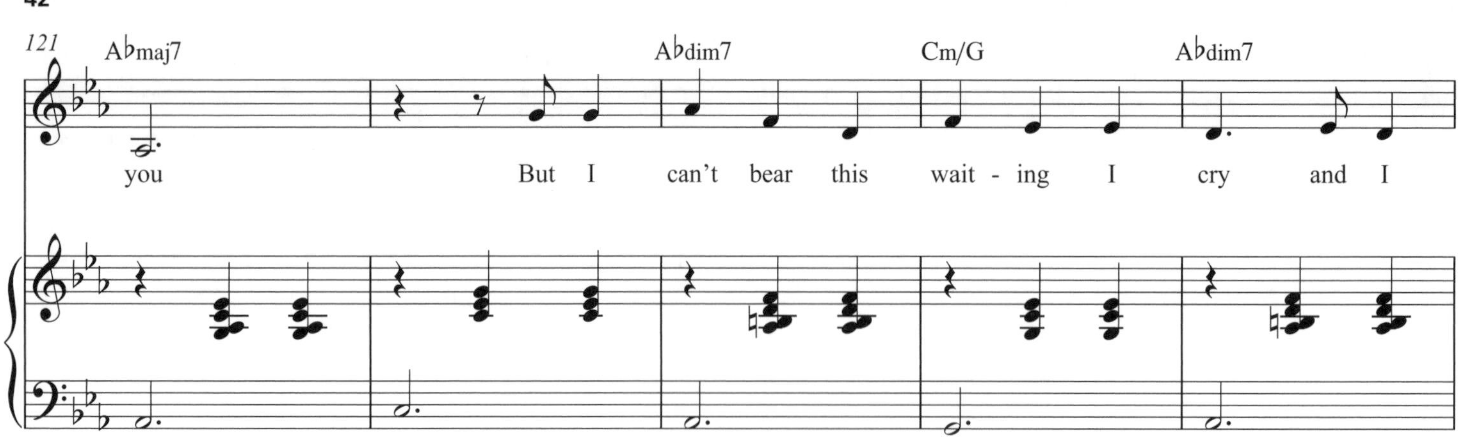
121
A♭maj7
A♭dim7
Cm/G
A♭dim7
you
But I can't bear this wait - ing I cry and I

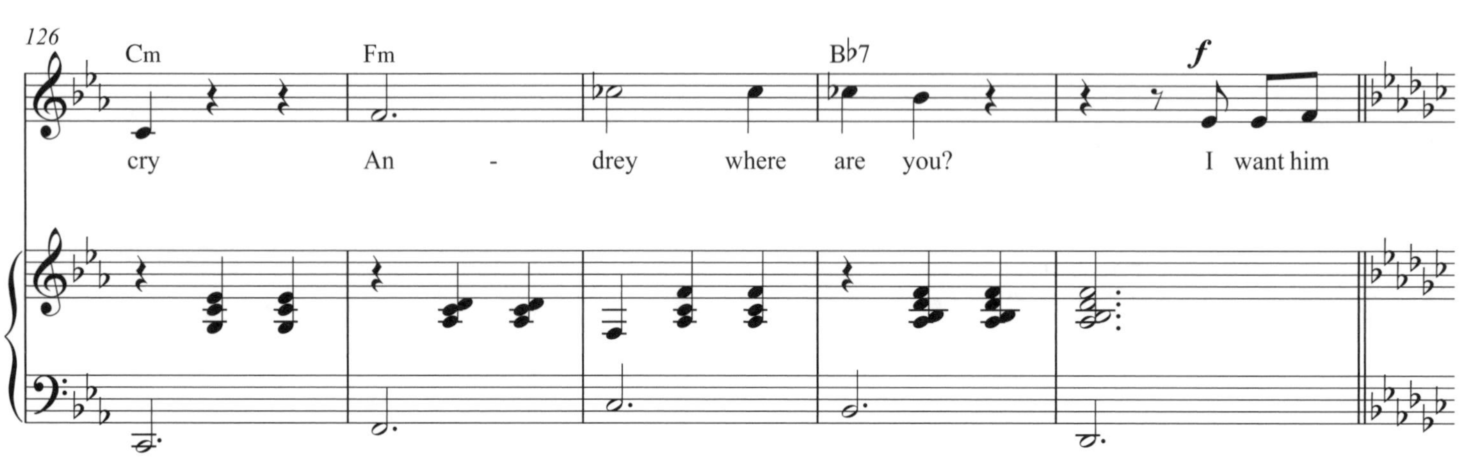
126
Cm
Fm
B♭7
f
cry An - drey where are you? I want him

131
E♭m
B♭7
E♭m
B♭7
A♭m
rit.
now, at once To em - brace him and cling to him No one can
f
rit.

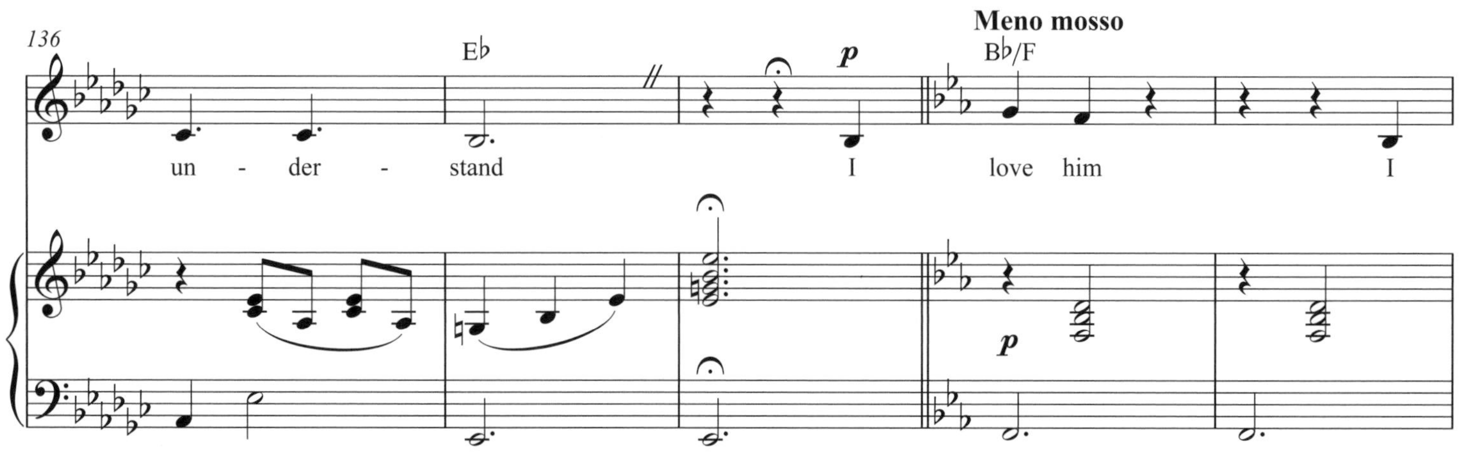
136
E♭
Meno mosso
B♭/F
p
un - der - stand I love him I
p

141
B♭7/F
B♭7♭9/F
E♭/B♭
know him He loves me on - ly He'll come
147
A♭m6
E♭/G
A♭m6
E♭/B♭
D7/F♯
home one day And take me a - way I want noth - ing
153
Gm
B♭7
E♭
more I want noth - ing more
159
B♭/F
B♭7/F
B♭7♭9/F
Hm
Hm

165
E♭/B♭
E♭
A♭m6
E♭/G
A♭m6
E♭/B♭
Hm
Hm
171
D7/F♯
Gm
B♭7
Hm
Hm
A tempo
177
E♭
A♭m
E♭/G
A♭m
E♭
MARYA D.: mp
First thing to - mor - row to Mad - ame Cham - bord's
mp
183
D♭
C7
4
Fm
Dres - ses, dres - ses we'll buy what we can af - ford
Then

188
B♭
B♭7
E♭
A♭m6
din - ner and a game of Bos - ton Then you'll read to
193
E♭
F7
F9
poco accel.
me while I knit How won - der - ful to have you
poco accel.
199
D7
NATASHA, SONYA: mf
here In - stead of these goss - ips and cry - ba - bies You'll
204
A tempo
B♭7
E♭
E♭9
A♭
take us where we must go Pet us a bit and
mf

209
Eb7b9
Ab
SONYA: D7/F#
Gm
scold us a bit Her god - daugh - ter, her fav - orite, Na - tash - a She will
215
Bb7
Eb
Abm
MARYA D.:
touch you on the cheek Well,
220
Eb7
Abm
Eb7
Abm
Eb7
now we'll talk I con - grat - u - late you and An - drey You've
225
Abm
Eb7
Abm
Eb7
Abm
hooked a fine fel - low! One of the fi - nest match - es in all of

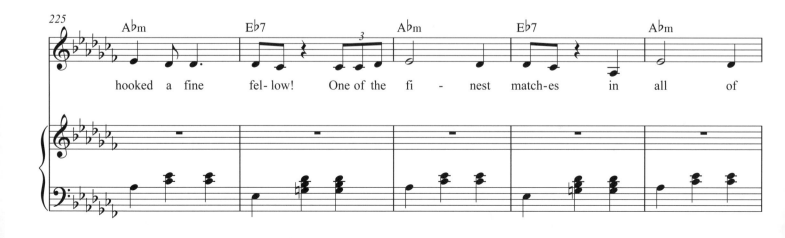

230
E♭7
D♭m6
Rus - sia I am glad and re - lieved He'll be the fam - ily's sav - ing
235
A♭m
NATASHA:
E♭7
A♭m
MARYA D.:
grace I blush hap - pi - ly But his fa - ther, Prince Bol -
240
E♭7
A♭m
E♭7
D♭m6
kon - sky, much dis - likes his son's marr - ying The old fel - low's
245
E♭7
crotch - et - y! Of course Prince An - drey's not a child But it's not nice

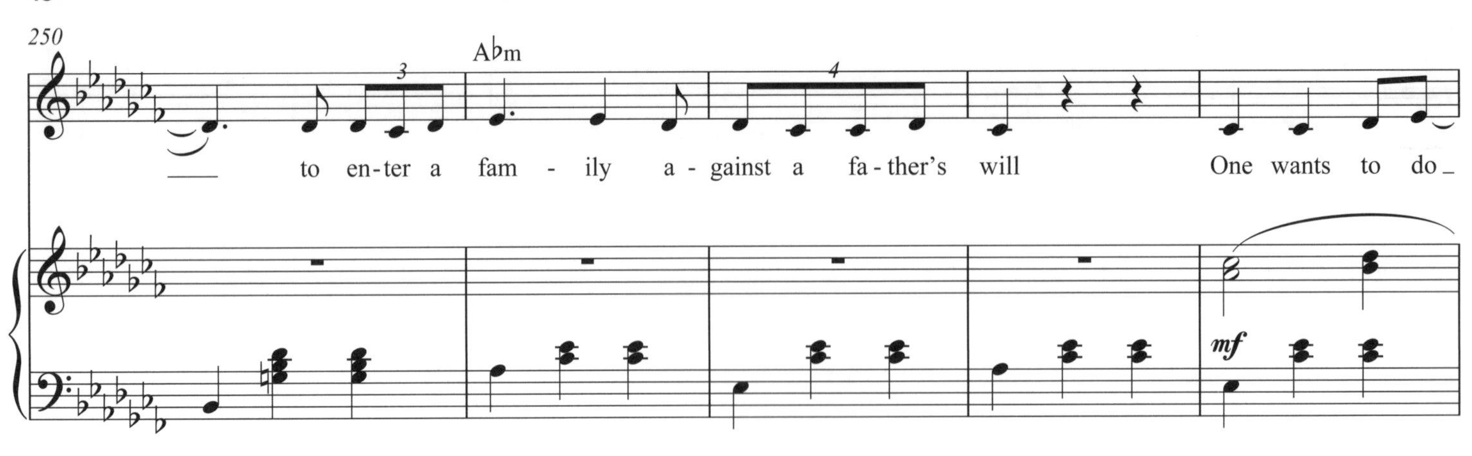
250
A♭m
to en-ter a fam - ily a - gainst a fa - ther's will
One wants to do
mf

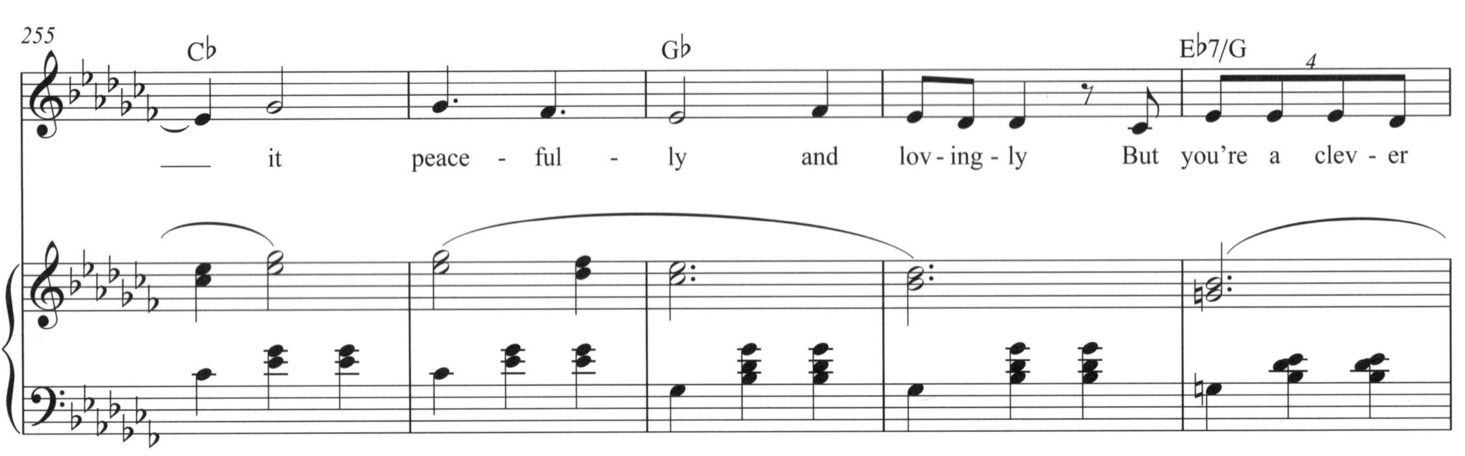
255
C♭
G♭
E♭7/G
it peace - ful - ly and lov - ing - ly
But you're a clev - er

260
A♭m
D♭m
girl Just be kind to An-drey's sis - ter, And when the sis - ter loves you
So will the

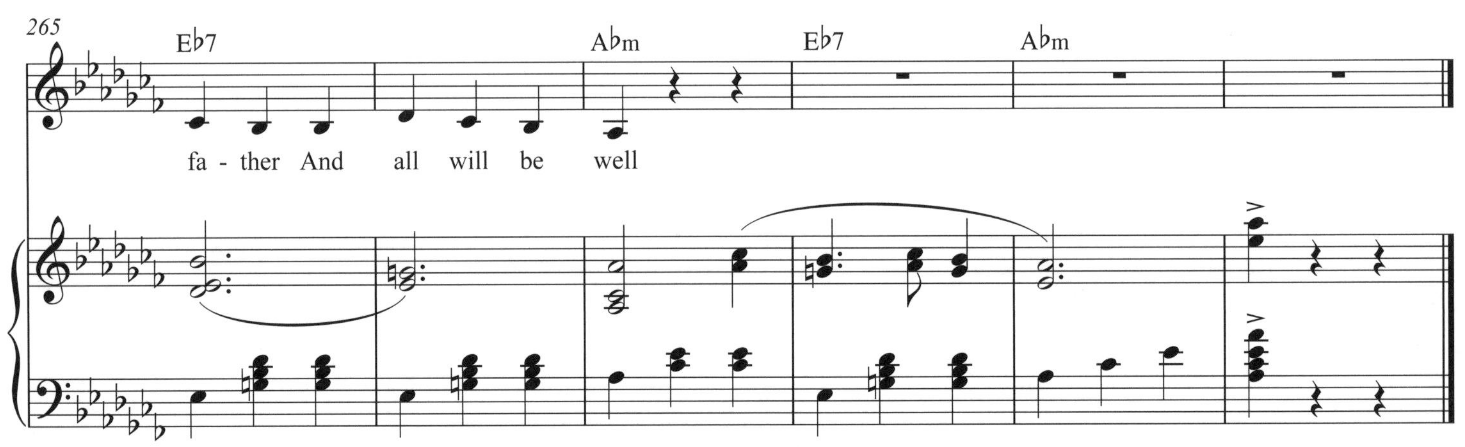
265
E♭7
A♭m
E♭7
A♭m
fa - ther And all will be well

NO ONE ELSE

Music and Lyrics by
DAVE MALLOY
Based on *War and Peace* by Leo Tolstoy

19
F
A7
Dm
B♭/D
mf
wide And the world was in - side of me
And I catch my
mf
23
F/C
B♭/D
F/C
Gm/B♭
F/A
C7/G
breath And I laugh and blush And I hear gui - tars
You are so good for
27
F
f
C11
me
I love you I love you I love you I love you I
f
31
C♯+
rall.
Tempo primo
Dm
B♭
mp
love you
Oh
rall.
mp

35
F
C♯+
Dm
B♭
the moon
39
F
C♯+
Dm
B♭
Oh
43
F
C♯+
Dm
B♭
the snow in the moon - light
47
F
C♯+
mf
Dm
B♭
And your child - like eyes And your

51
F
C♯+
Dm
B♭
dis - tant smile I'll nev - er be this hap - py a - gain
55
F
C11
You and I
59
rit.
p
F
a tempo
And no one else
rit.
a tempo
Faster
63
C♯+
rall.
Gm
D7/F♯
B♭/F
mf
We've done this all be - fore We were
rall.
mf

67
Em7♭5
rall.
B♭/D
a tempo
an - gels once Don't you re-mem - ber? Joy and
8va
rall.
a tempo
71
C7
B♭/D
C7
B♭/D
C7
Gm/B♭
F/A
life In - side our souls And no - bo - dy knows Just you and me
75
C7/G
F
mf
C7
It's our se - cret This win - ter
79
F
F7
B♭
f
C7/B♭
sky How can an - y - one sleep? There was nev-er such a night be -
f

83
F
F7
B♭
Bm(maj7)
G7/B
F/C
B♭m/D♭
fore!
I feel like put-ting my arms 'round my knees
And squeez - ing tight as
mf
87
Dm
B♭
sub. p
rall.
Tempo primo
F
pos - si - ble
And fly - ing a - way
8va
ff
sub. p
rall.
mp
91
C7
Like this...
95
C♯+
Dm
mf
Oh
mf

99
B♭
F
C♯+
Dm
the
moon
103
B♭
F
C♯+
Dm
Oh
107
B♭
F
C♯+
Dm
the
snow
in
the
moon
-
light
111
B♭
F
C♯+
Dm
And
your
child
-
like

115 B♭ F C♯+ Dm

eyes And your dis - tant smile_ I'll nev - er be this

119 B♭ F *mf* C11

hap - py a - gain___ You and I___

mf

123

f

You and I___

accel e molto cresc.

f

127

ff

You and I___

ff

131
sub. p molto rit.
Dm
a tempo
And no one else
molto rit.
mp a tempo
Molto rubato (♪ = 100)
(♩ = ♪)
135
B♭
F
C♯+
Dm
pp
May - be he'll come to - day
pp
139
F/E♭
Dm
C♯(♭5)
F/C
May - be he came al - read - y And he's sit - ting in the
143
G7/B
B♭m6
F/A
F
draw ing room And I simp - ly for - got
p

DUST AND ASHES

Music and Lyrics by
DAVE MALLOY
Based on *War and Peace* by Leo Tolstoy

Slow dirge (♩. = 66)

Gm(add4) D7♯5/F♯ Gm(add4)

pp

4 D7♯5/F♯ Gm(add4) D7♯5/F♯

PIERRE: *p*

Is this how I die? Rid - i - culed _ and laughed at Wear-ing

Gm(add4) D7♯5/F♯ Gm(add4)

7

clown shoes _ Is this how I die? _

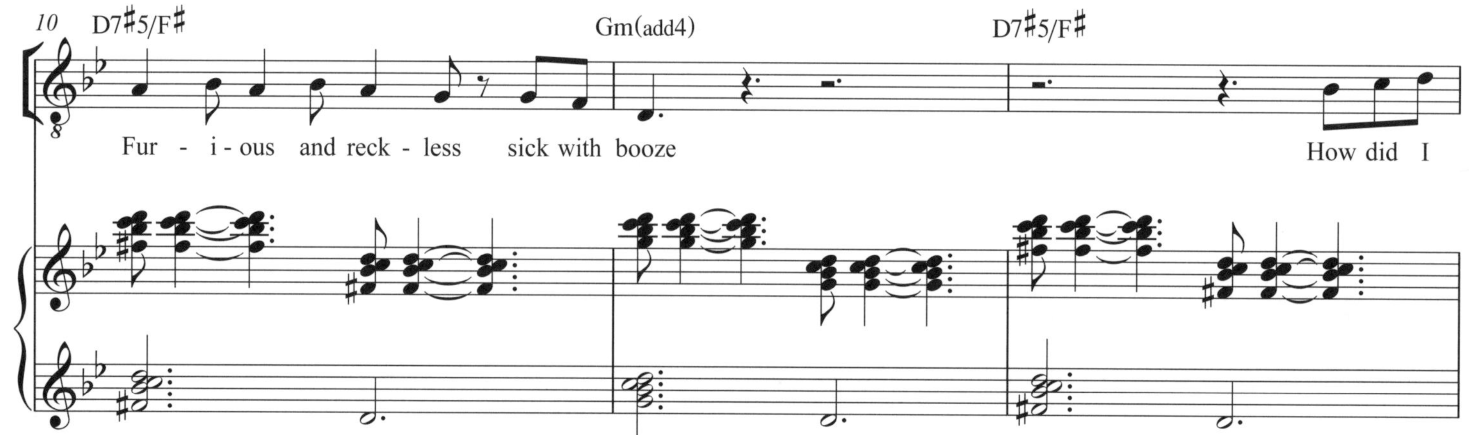

13
Eb6/G
Eb6
F7/Eb
Bb/D
Bb7
live? I taste ev - ery wast - ed min-ute Ev-ery - time I turned a -
16
Eb(add2)
Cm(add4)
way From the things that might have
18
Ebm6
Bbmaj7/D
Eb(add2)
mp
healed me How long have I been sleep-ing Is this how I
21
Gm(add4)
D7#5/F#
die? Fright - ened like a chi - ld La - zy and
mp
sempre legato; very quiet offbeats,
just to give it a little rocking motion

23 Gm(add4) D7♯5/F♯ Cm11

numb Is this how I die? Pre-

26 E♭m(maj7) E♭m6 Gm(add4)

tend - ing and pre - pos - ter - ous and dumb

28 Gm(add4) E♭(add2)

How did I live? Was I

sim.

30 F7/E♭ B♭/D B♭7

kind e - nough and good e - nough? Did I love e

32
E♭(add2)
Cm(add4)
nough?
Did I e - ver look up and see the
34
E♭m6
B♭/F
E♭m6/G♭
moon and the stars and the sky?
Oh why have I been
A little bit faster (♩. = 78)
36
B♭(add2)
B♭7
E♭
D7
rit.
mf
sleep - ing?
They say we are a - sleep Un - til we
mp
rit.
38
Gm
B♭7
E♭
D7
Gm
fall in love We are chil - dren of dust and ash - es
But

poco più mosso
41
Cm11
F7
D7/F♯
Gm
E♭
when we fall in love we wake up And we are a God and an - gels
f
a tempo
44
B♭/F
E♭
B♭/F
weep But if I die here to - night I
pp
47
F7
B♭
rit.
D7/F♯
die in my sleep
rit.
Poco accelerando
Am6
Am
50
Gm
Gm6
Am6
Gm
B♭+
B♭+
C
D/C
mp
All of my life I spent search-ing the words of po - ets and saints and proph-ets and kings And
mp

52
Gm Gm6 Am6 Am6/Gm Am/B♭+ B♭+ C D/C
mp
mf
now at the end all I know that I've learned is that all that I know is I don't know a thing So
mp
Allegretto (♩. = 100)
54
E♭ B♭ D7 Gm
eas - y to close off Place the blame_ out - side_
mf sparkling
56
E♭ B♭ D7 Gm
Hid - ing_ in my room at night so terr - i - fied_
58
Gm D7/F♯ A♭/E♭ E♭
all the things I could have been but I nev - er had_ the nerve_

60
D7
Gm
B♭/F
F7
B♭
G7/B
accel.
f
Life and love I don't de - serve So all
accel.
Barroom stomp (♩. = 100)
62
Cm
G7
A♭
E♭
D7
Gm
Cm/E♭
right, all right, I've had my time Close my eyes let the
f
65
B♭/F
F7
B♭
G7/B
Cm
Gmaj7
death bells chime Bur - y me in bur - gun - dy I
67
A♭
E♭
D7
Gm
Cm/E♭
just don't care Noth - ing's left I looked

Raucous; a la New Orleans funeral march
69
B♭/F F7 B♭ ff D7/F♯
ev - ery - where Is this how I
Gm Gm/D
die? Was there
ff solo ad lib!
71
D7♯5/F♯ D7
ev - er an - y oth - er way my life could
Gm Gm/D
be?
73
D7♯5/F♯ Dm7♯5
Is this how I
Cm7 Cm7/G
die? Such a
75
E♭m(maj7) E♭m(maj7)/G♭
storm of feel - ings in -
Gm Gm/D
side of me

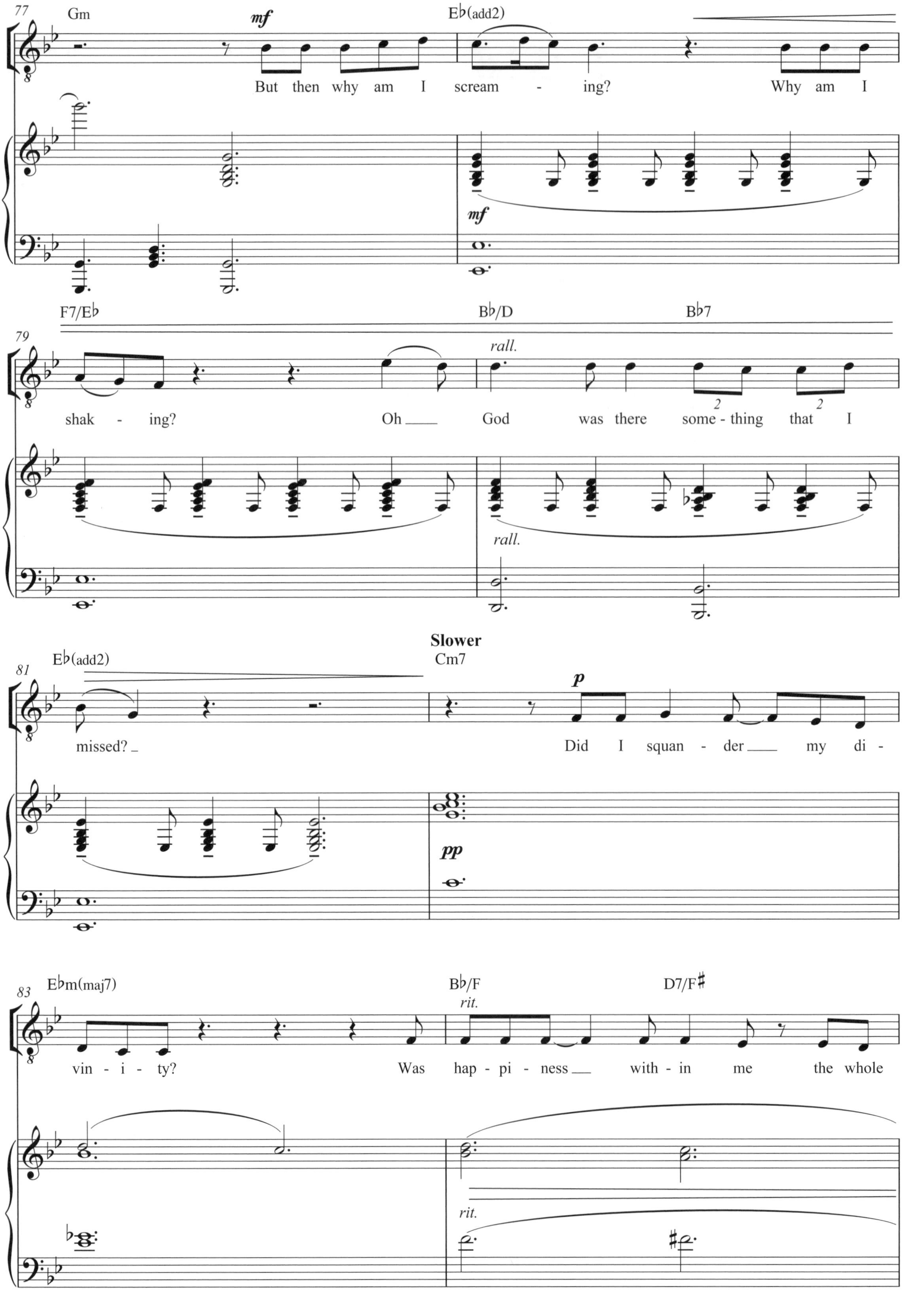

77 Gm *mf* E♭(add2)

But then why am I scream - ing? Why am I

mf

79 F7/E♭ B♭/D B♭7

rall.

shak - ing? Oh ___ God was there some - thing that I

rall.

81 E♭(add2) **Slower** Cm7

p

missed? _ Did I squan - der ___ my di -

pp

85

Gm

mf

Allargando (♩. = 82)

time? They say we are a-sleep Un-til we fall in love We are

CHORUS: *mf*

Ah

CHORUS: *mf*

Ah

mf *piano reduction (in absence of chorus)*

88

poco più mosso

chil-dren of dust and ash-es But when we fall in love we wake

Ah Ah Ah

Ah Ah

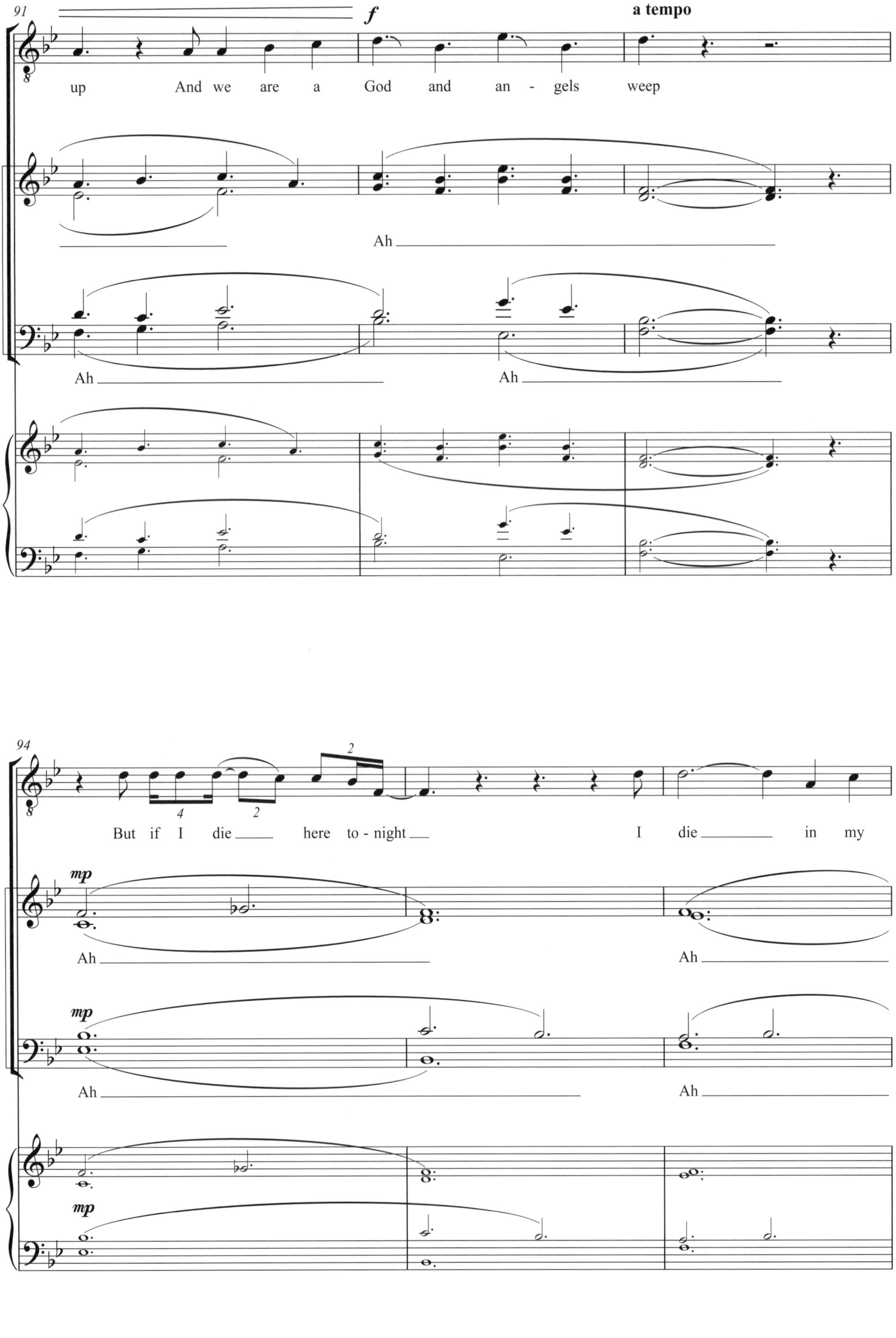

91

f

a tempo

up And we are a God and an - gels weep

Ah

Ah Ah

94

But if I die here to - night I die in my

mp

Ah Ah

mp

Ah Ah

mp

più mosso
meno mosso
Molto allargando
97
B♭
B♭maj7
B♭7
ff
E♭
D7
sleep
They say we are a-sleep un-til we
ff
Ah
Ah
Ah
ff
Ah
Ah
mf
f
100
Gm
B♭7(add4)
fall in love
and I'm so

Driving (♩. = 110)
103
E♭
E♭m(maj7)
f
read-y to wake up now
I want to wake
mp
106
B♭7/D
E♭m6
B♭/F
E♭m6/G♭ A♭(add2)
B♭7/D
E♭m6
up
Don't let me die while I'm like this
f
109
B♭/F
E♭m6/G♭ A♭(add2)
B♭7/D
E♭m6
B♭/F
E♭m6/G♭ A♭(add2)
I want to wake up
God don't let me die while I'm like
112
B♭7/D
E♭m6
B♭/F
E♭m6/G♭ A♭(add2)
B♭7/D
E♭m6
molto cresc.
this
Please let me wake up now
God
molto cresc.

115
B♭/F
E♭m6/G♭
A♭(add2)
Adim7
E♭m6/B♭
E♭m6/C
__ don't let me die while I'm _ like this
I'm
sempre molto cresc.
118
B♭7/D
E♭m6
B♭7/F
E♭m6/G♭
A♭13♯11
E♭m6/B♭
read-y __
I'm
read-y __
Molto allargando
121
E♭m6/C
B♭9/D
C♭7/E♭
ff
To wake
ff
124
B♭
E♭m6
B♭
E♭m6
Cdim7
B♭
up __
ff
mp
ff

CHARMING

Music and Lyrics by
DAVE MALLOY
Based on *War and Peace* by Leo Tolstoy

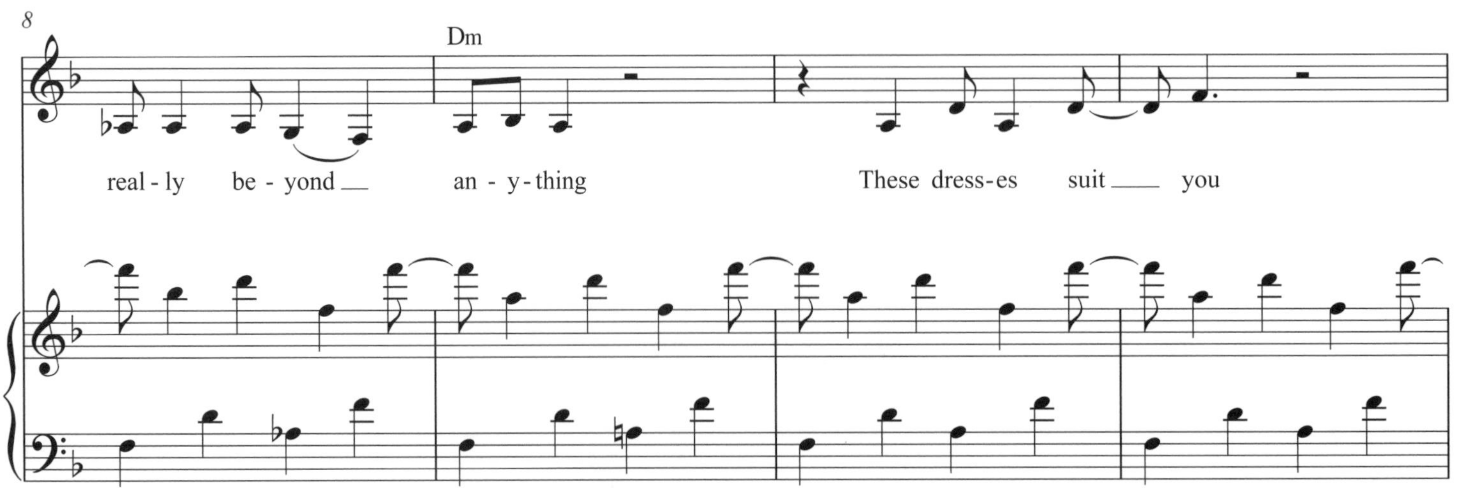

12
B♭7
This one, "met - al - lic gauze"
Straight from Par - is
15
Dm
mf
An - y-thing suits you, my charm - er
Oh how she
f
19
A7
Dm
Dm
A7
blush - es, how she blush - es, my pret - ty!
Oh how she blush - es, how she blush - es, my pret -
mp
22
Dm
Gm
D
- ty! Char - man - te, char - man - te!
You are such a love - ly thing Oh

25 Fm C Dm A7 Dm

where have you been? It's such a shame to bur - y pearls in the coun - try Char-man - te, char-man - te,

28

mf

charm - ing Now if you have a dress You must

mf

31 B♭7

wear it out How can you live in Mos -

34 Dm

3

- cow and not go no - where? So you

37
B♭7
love some - bod - y, charm-ing But that's no rea - son to shut your-self
40
in E-ven if you're en-gaged You must wear your dress out
43
Dm
mp
Bm7♭5
some - where My broth-er dined with me yes - ter - day
mp
46
B♭7
Bm7♭5
B♭7
But he did - n't eat a thing Cuz he was think - ing 'bout

49
mf
you He kept sigh - ing 'bout you
Oh how she
f
52
Dm
A7♭9
Dm
A7♭9
blush - es, how she blush - es, my pret - ty!
Oh how she blush - es, how she blush - es, my pret -
mf
55
Dm
Gm
D
- ty! Char - man - te, char - man - te!
You are such a love - ly thing Oh
58
Fm
C
Dm
A7
Dm
where have you been? It's such a shame to bur - y pearls in the coun - try Char - man - te, char - man - te,

61
f
charm-ing
Now a wom-an with a dress
Is a
mf
64
B♭7
fright-ening and po-wer-ful
thing
You are not a child When you're
67
Dm
draped in scar-let and lace
Your fi-an-cé would
71
B♭7
want you to have fun
Rath-er than be bored to death

74
Dm
All - i - ez dans la monde Plu - tôt que de dé - pé - rir d' en - nui
77
mf
Bm7♭5
B♭7
My broth - er is quite mad - ly in love He is quite
mf
80
Bm7♭5
B♭7
mad - ly in love with you, my dear
83
ff
Dm
A7♭9
Ho Oh how she blush - es, how she blush - es, my pret -
ff

86
Dm
Dm
A7
Dm
- ty! Oh how she blush-es, how she blush-es, my pret - ty! Char-man-te, char-man-te!
89
Gm
D
Fm
C
You are such a love-ly thing Oh where have you been? It's such a
92
Dm
A7♭9
Dm
mp
shame to bur-y pearls in the coun - try Char man-te, char-man-te, charm-ing It's such a
gliss.
95
Dm
A7♭9
Dm
shame to bur-y pearls in the coun - try Char-man-te, char-man-te, charm-ing
p
f

THE BALL

Music and Lyrics by
DAVE MALLOY
Based on *War and Peace* by Leo Tolstoy

♩ = 123

D7

mf

ANATOLE:

5 *mf*

Wait-ing at the door Wait-ing at the door Wait - ing

9

Wait-ing at the door Wait-ing at the door Wait - ing How I a -

13

dore lit - tle girls ________ They lose their heads at

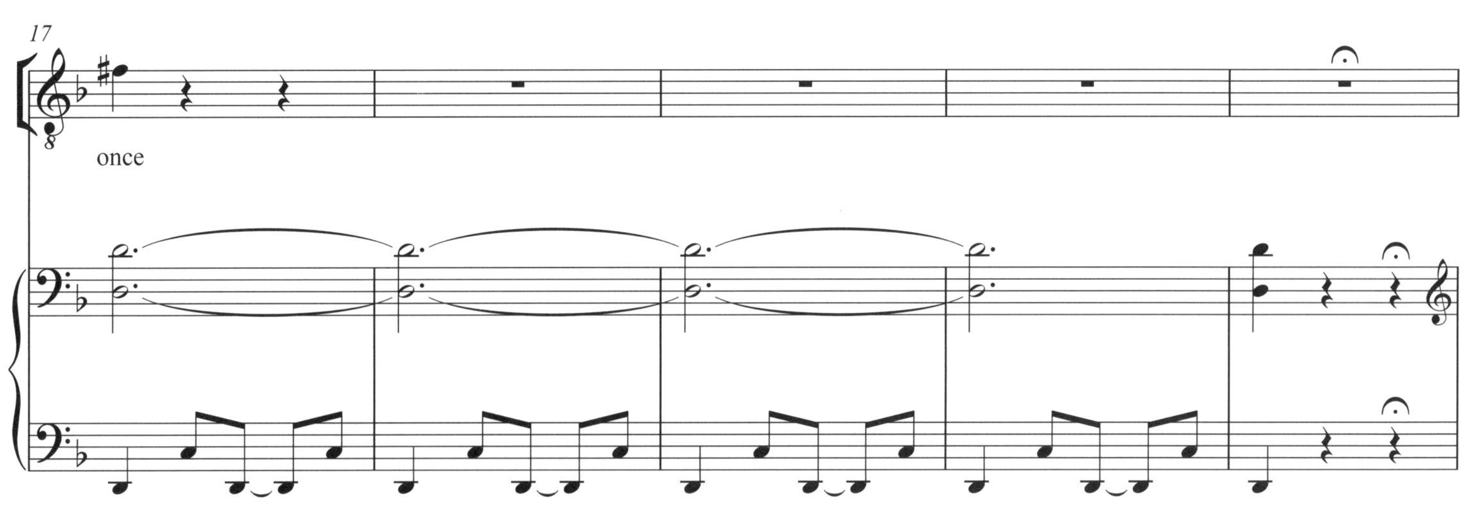
17
once

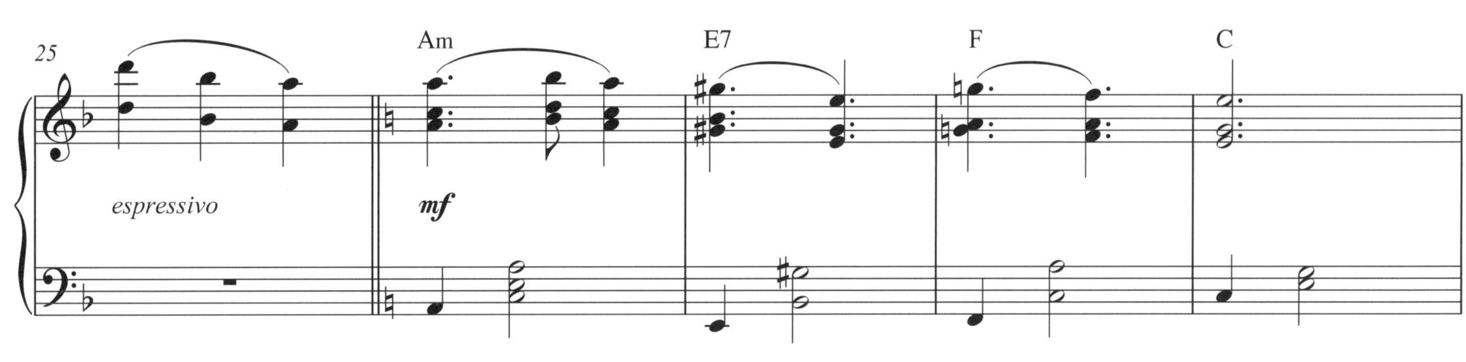
25
Am
E7
F
C
espressivo
mf

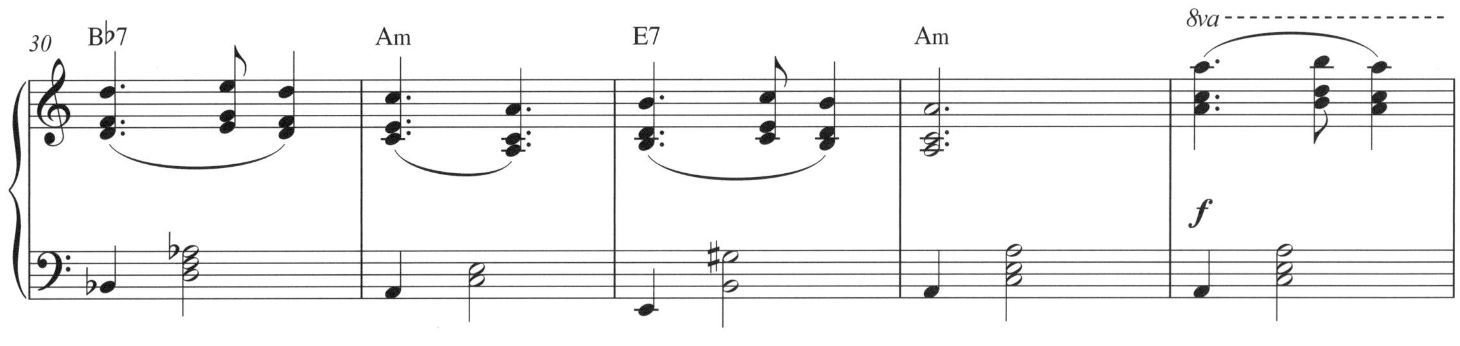
30
B♭7
Am
E7
Am
8va
f

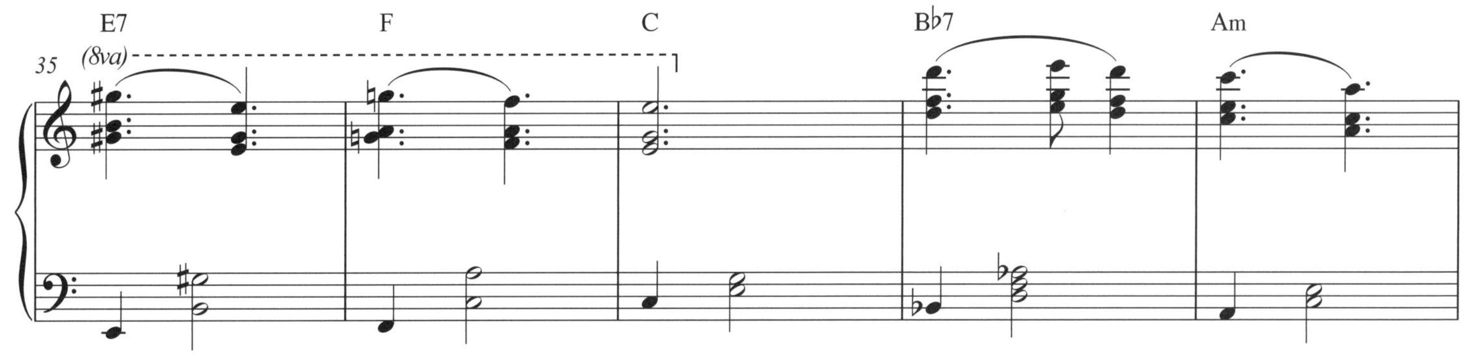
E7
F
C
B♭7
Am
35
(8va)

E7
Am

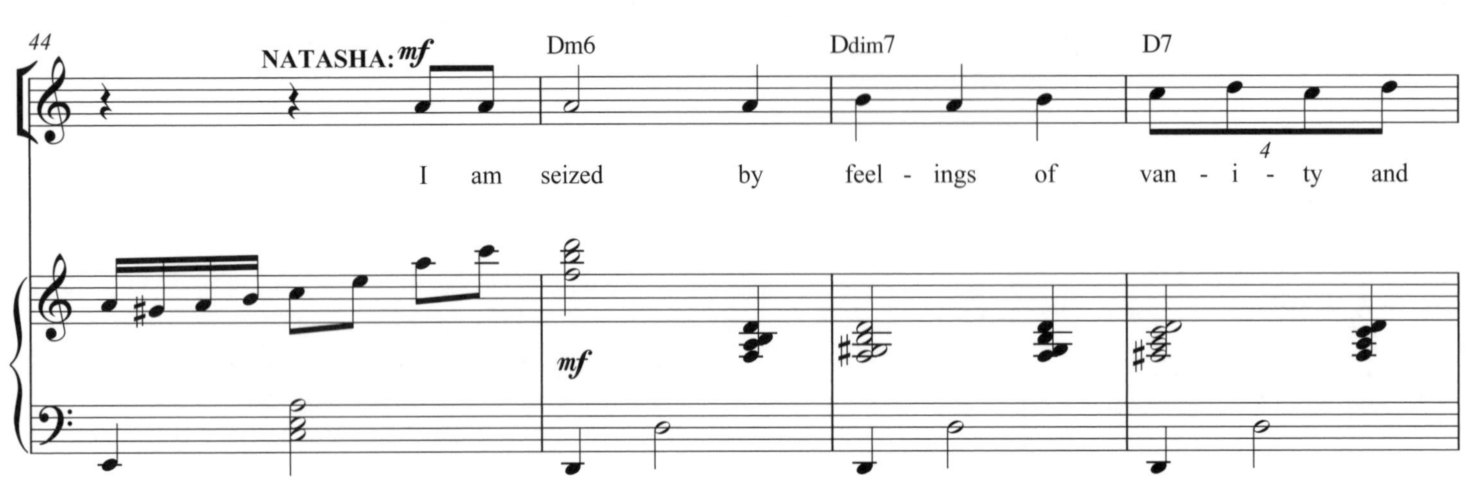
NATASHA: mf
Dm6
Ddim7
D7
I am seized by feel - ings of van - i - ty and
mf

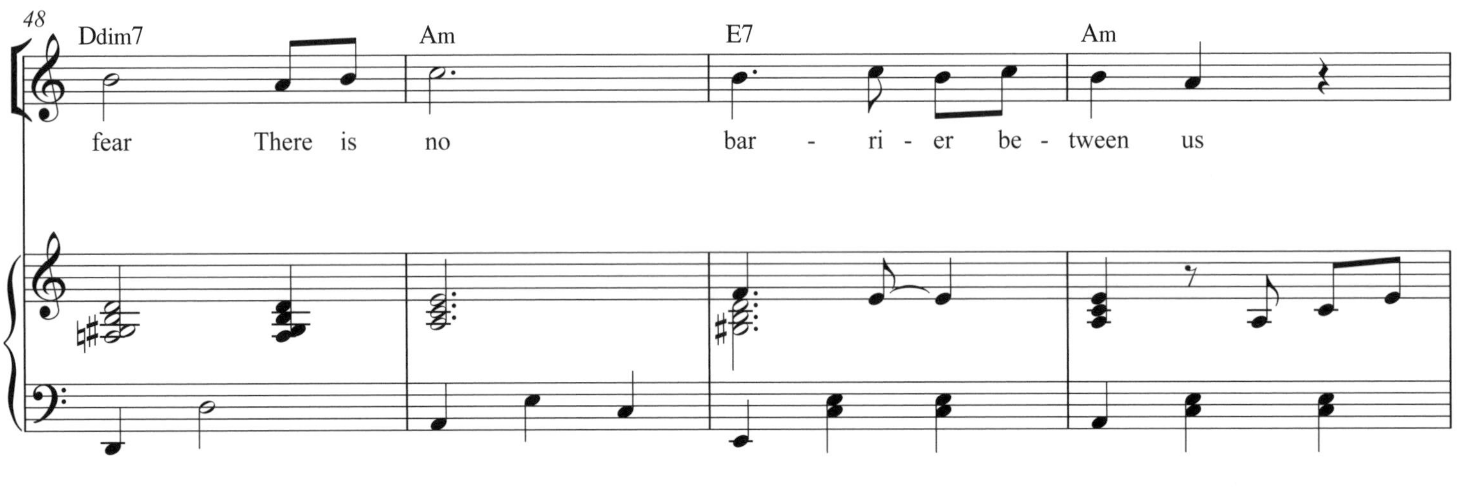
Ddim7
Am
E7
Am
fear There is no bar - ri - er be - tween us

Dm6
Ddim7
D7
Whis - pers and moans and ring - ing in my

56
Ddim7
Am
E7
Am
ear There is no bar - ri - er be - tween us
60
Gm9
Fmaj7
Di - vine, de - li - cious But I do not
64
B/F
Em9
see or hear an - y - thing
68
Cmaj7
B/C
I'm borne a - way to a sense - less

72
B♭
A♭
Am
world So strange, so re - mote
76
Esus
Em
I don't know good from bad
80
Dm
C
An - a - tole An - a - tole
84
B7
Em
I'm so fright - ened

89
C/E
C7/E
NATASHA:
Fm
And as we danced he
ANATOLE:
You are en - chant - ing
94
pressed my waist and hand And told me I was Be -
Be -
99
B♭m6
witch - ing
Be -
witch - ing And I love you
Be -

103

witch - ing

witch - ing And I love you

107

Fm

And dur - ing the ec - cos - sai - se, he gazed in my

Gaze in my

111

B♭m6

eyes And said noth - ing, just gazed in my eyes My

eyes Gaze in my eyes

115
fright - ened eyes

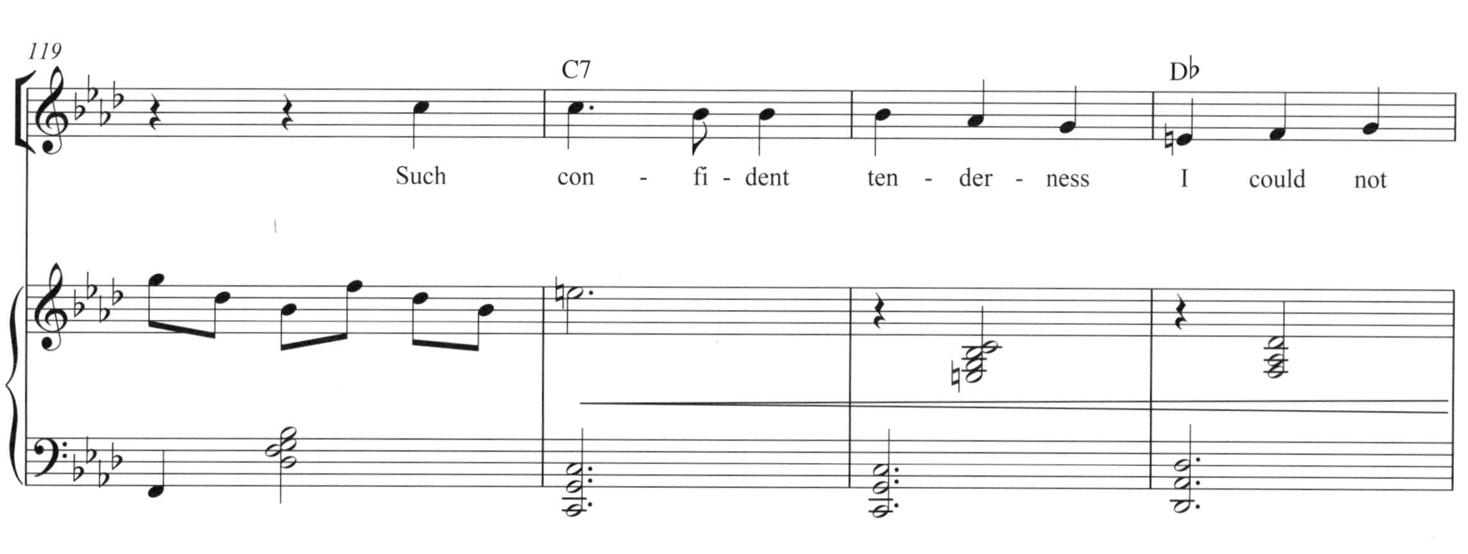
119
C7
Db
Such con - fi - dent ten - der - ness I could not

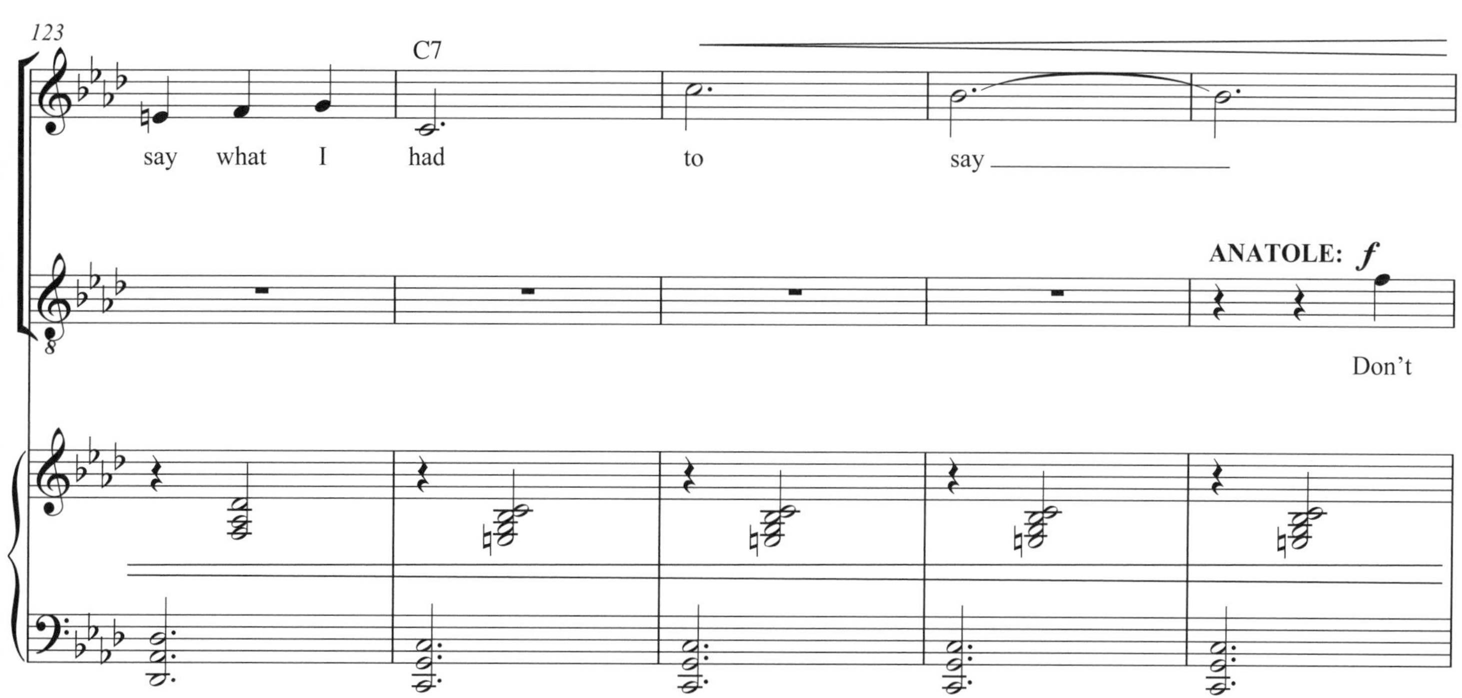
123
C7
say what I had to say
ANATOLE: f
Don't

128
Fm
C7
D♭
A♭
G♭
low - er your eyes
I love you
I am in
f

133
Fm
C7
Fm
C7
love dear
I am in
love
Gaze in my
eyes

138
D♭
A♭
G♭
Fm
C7
I love
you
You are be - witch - ing
What can I

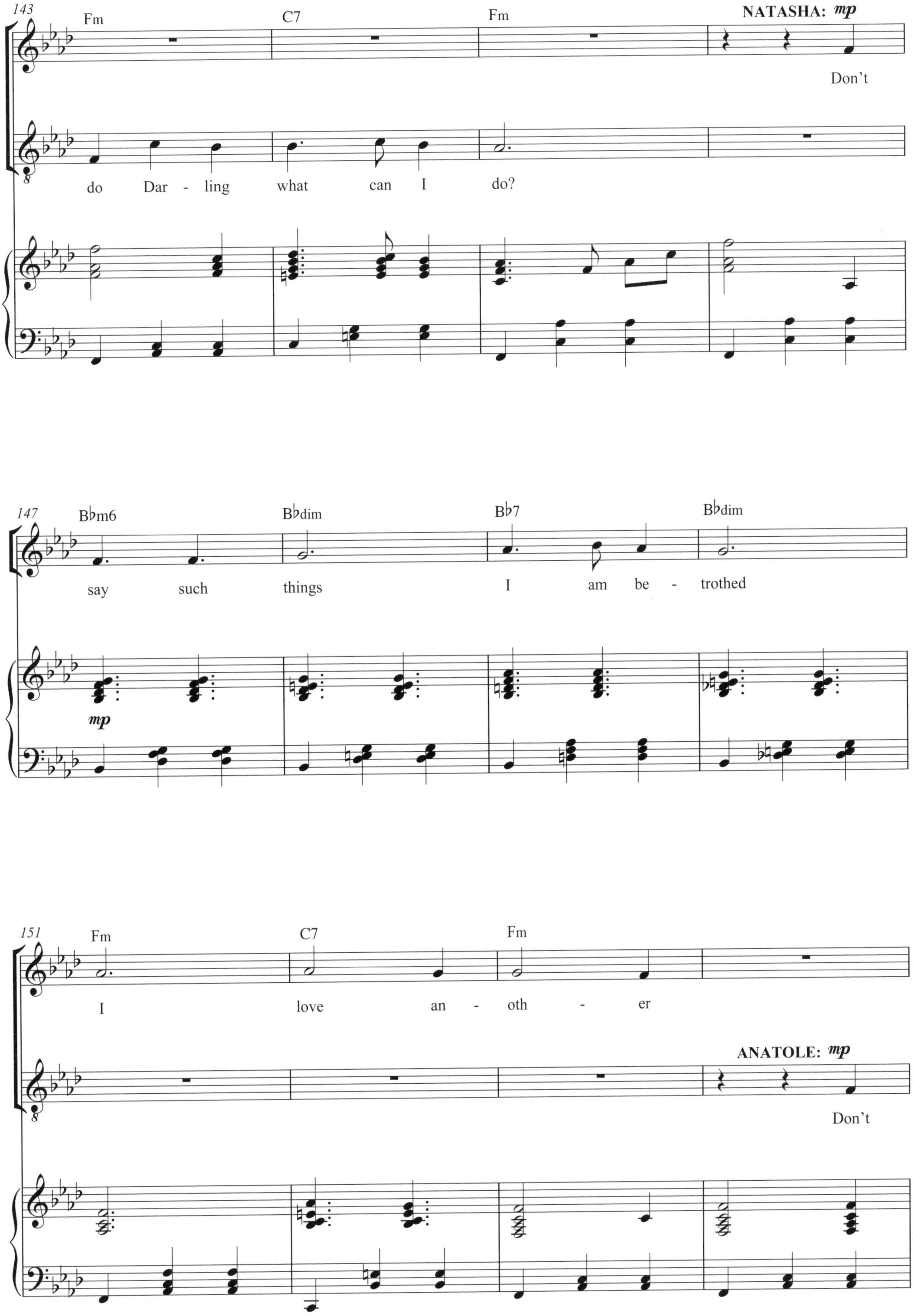

143
Fm C7 Fm
NATASHA: *mp*
Don't
do Dar - ling what can I do?

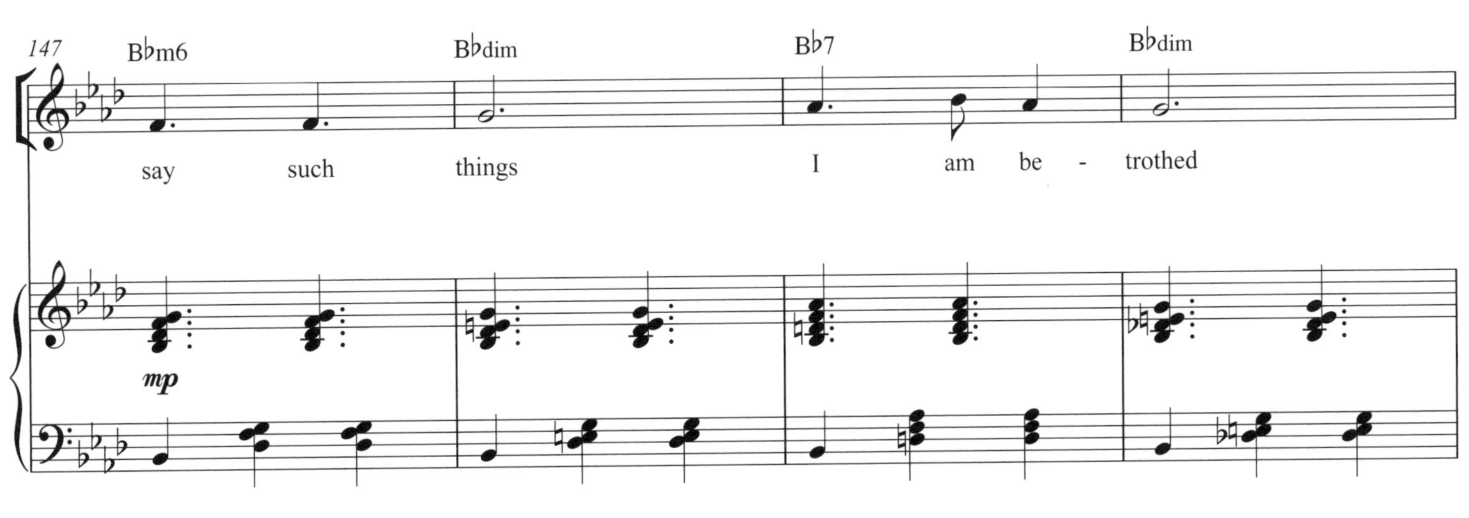

155
B♭m6
B♭dim
B♭7
B♭dim
speak to me of that! When I tell you that I am

159
Fm
C7
Fm
mad - ly, mad - ly, in love with you! Is it

163
E♭m9
D♭maj7
my fault that you're en - chant - ing?

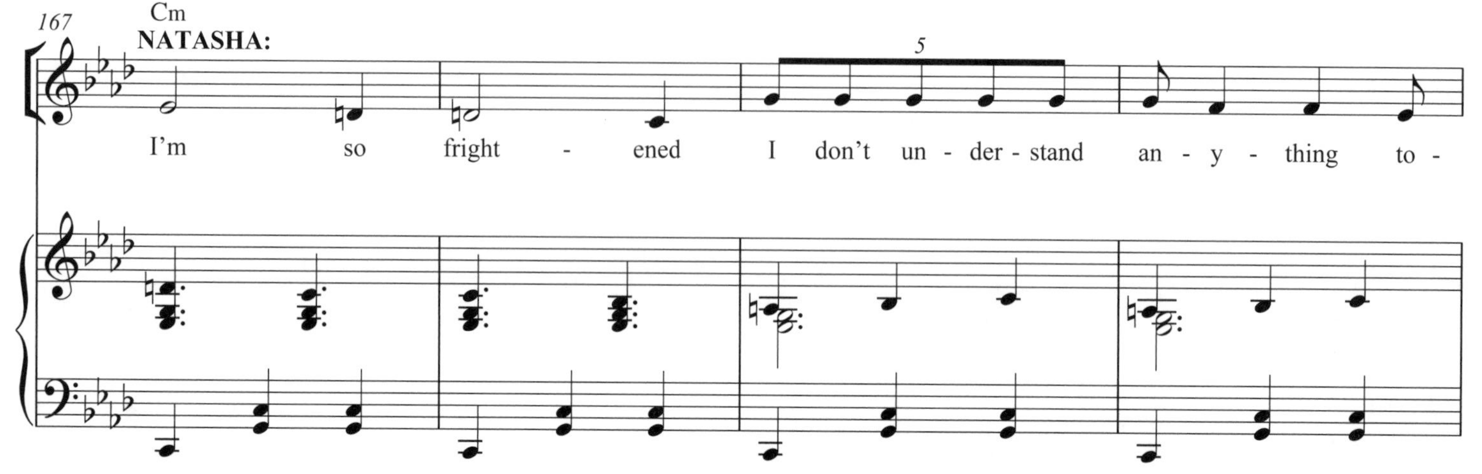
167
Cm
NATASHA:
5
I'm so fright - ened I don't un - der - stand an - y - thing to -

171

A♭ A♭dim7

night

ANATOLE:

I'm here now

Hit piano top

ff

176

ANATOLE:

Na - ta - lie!

Repeat 6 bar phrase until Anatole lunges; then go on to m. 203

Freely; speech rhythm (but intense)

185
His large,
path, I bring her face close to mine

188
3
3
glit - ter - ing, mas - cu - line eyes are so close to mine That I see noth - ing else

191
3
Is it pos - si - ble that I should nev - er see you a - gain? I love you mad - ly!

194
You press my arm
Can I nev - er? Nat - a - lie? Nat - a - lie?

198
You're hurt - ing my hands I don't un - der-stand
Nat - a - lie?

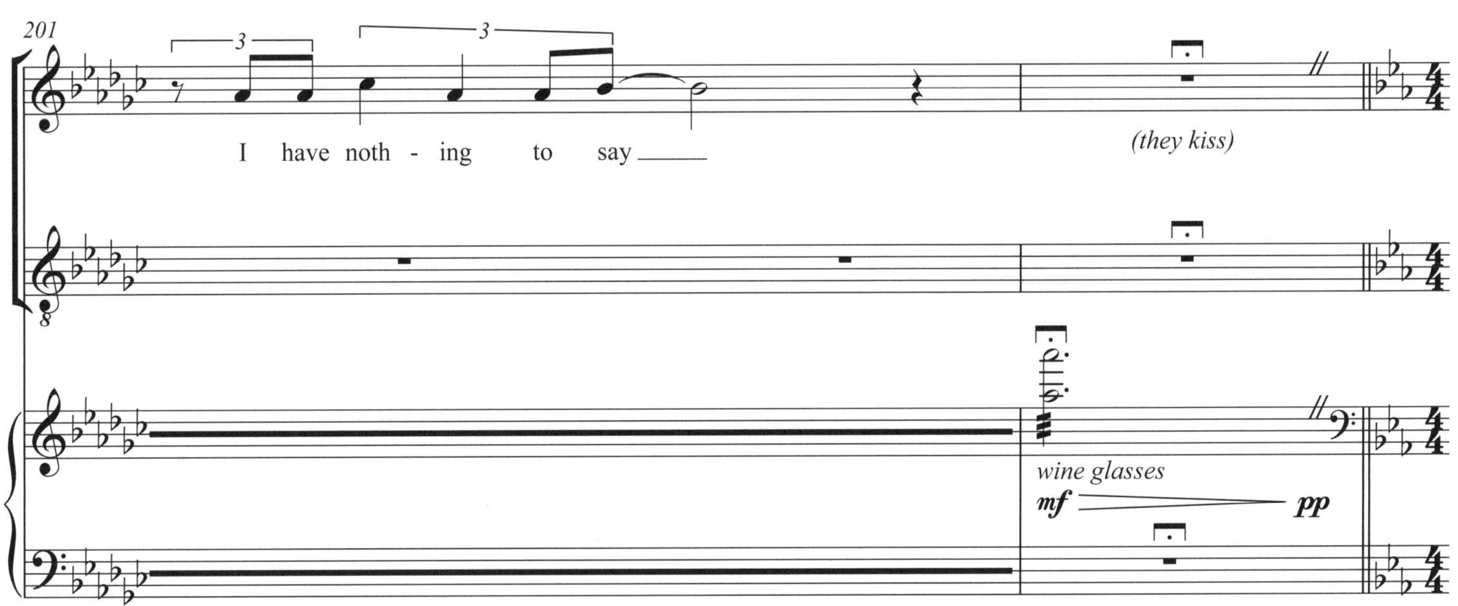
201
I have noth - ing to say
(they kiss)
wine glasses
mf
pp

Much slower
204
Cm Bb Ab Cm Bb Ab
NATASHA: mp
Burn-ing lips pressed to mine Tell me what just hap - pened I'm
mp
208
Fm7 Fdim7 F
p
trem - bling So fright - ening An - drey But I
212
F/C F7b9/C
love you Of that there
p
217
Bb/F Bb Ebm6
is no doubt How else could all of this have
4

222
B♭
E♭m6
B♭
hap - pened?
How else could we have kissed? _
227
mp
D7/F♯
4
Gm
It means _ that I have loved you from the first
mp
231
D7/F♯
It means _ that you are kind, no - ble, and
235
mf
Gm
E♭
B♭
rit.
splen - did And I could not help lov - ing you
rit.

240
Gm
F
E♭7
I will love you An - a - tole
CHORUS:
CHORUS:
Ah
244
Gm
F
E♭7
I'll do an - y - thing for you
Ah
Ah

248

ff

Gm F E♭7 *rall.*

I'll do an - y - thing for you

ff

I'll do an - y - thing for you

ff

Ah

ff

Ah

ff

rall.

258

261

264

267
fff

270
F♭
C♭
G+
A♭m

LETTERS

Music and Lyrics by
DAVE MALLOY
Based on *War and Peace* by Leo Tolstoy

12
hap-pening in our minds Once it's on the pa - per we feel bet - ter We feel bet - ter It's
hap-pening in our minds Once it's on the pa - per we feel bet - ter We feel bet - ter It's

15
PIERRE: mf
Dear
like some kind of clar - i - ty When the let - ter's done and signed
like some kind of clar - i - ty When the let - ter's done and signed

17
3
An - drey Dear old friend How goes the war? Do we

19
march on the French splen-did- ly? Do our
3
21
can - nons crack and cry? Do our bul - lets whis - tle and sing? Does the
23
air reek with smoke? I wish I were
25
Dm
there With death at my heels
mf

27 Am

Do-lo-khov is re-cov-er-ing He will be all right _ the good man And Na-

EQUAL MIXED GROUPS: *mp*

Ha Ha

EQUAL MIXED GROUPS: *mp*

Ha Ha

29 Dm

tash - a ___ is in town _ Your bride-to-be, ___ so full of life ___ and mis - chief _ I should vis - it I

Ha ha ha ha ha ha Ha

Ha ha ha ha ha ha Ha

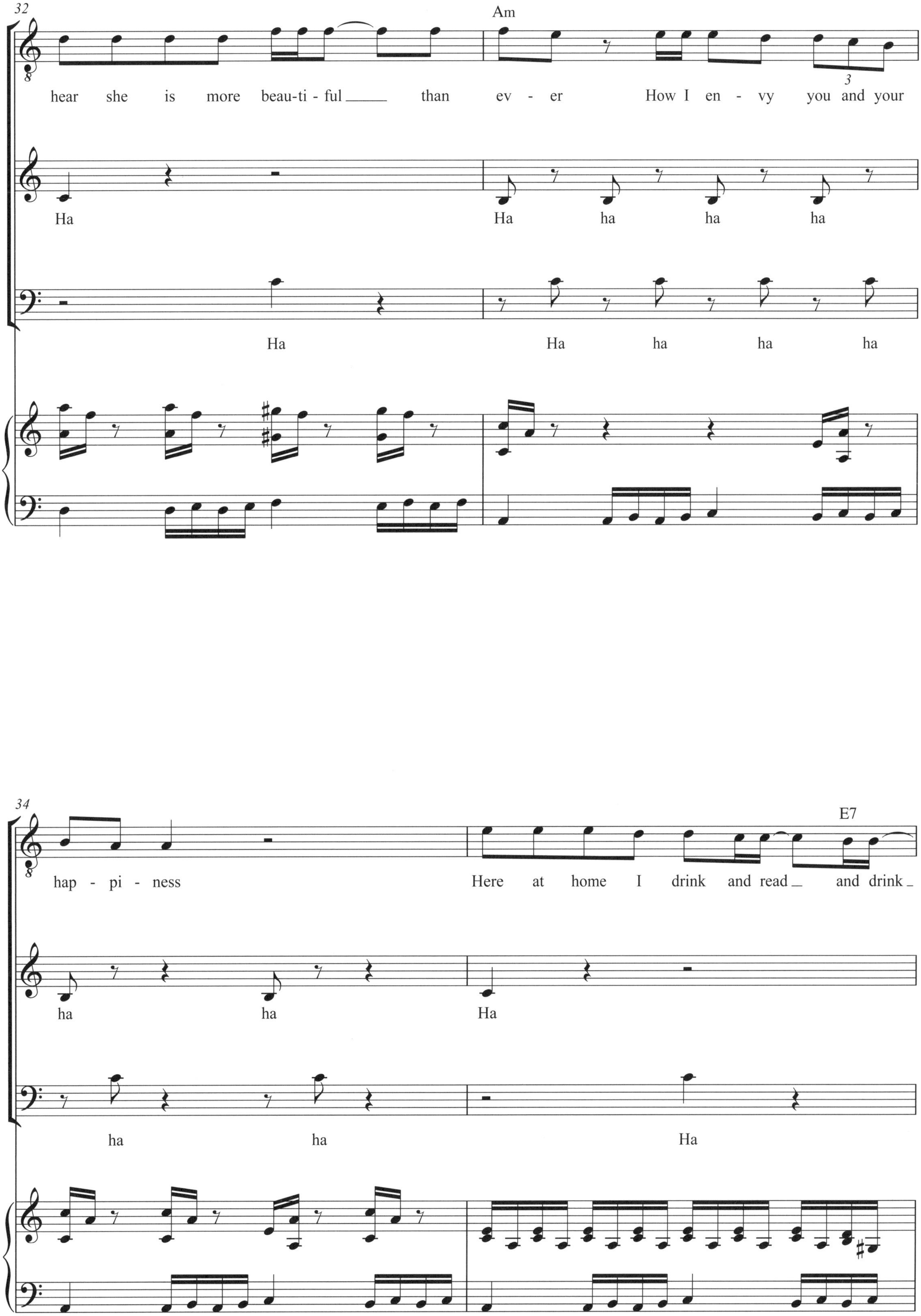

32

Am

hear she is more beau-ti-ful ___ than ev - er How I en - vy you and your

3

Ha

Ha ha ha ha

Ha

Ha ha ha ha

34
E7
hap - pi - ness
Here at home I drink and read _ and drink _
ha ha Ha
ha ha
Ha

36 Am E7

___ and read ___ and drink But I think I fin - ally found ___ it What my ___

Ha Ha ha ha

Ha Ha ha

38 Am E♭dim

f *mf*

___ heart has need - ed For I've been stud-ying the Ka - bal And I've cal -

mf

ha ha ha ha ha ha ha ha ha

mf

ha ha ha ha ha ha ha ha

40
Em Bbdim Bm Fdim

- cu - lat - ed the num - ber of the beast It is Na - pol - e - on

ha ha ha ha ha ha ha ha ha ha ha ha

ha ha ha ha ha ha ha ha

42
F#m Cdim C#m Gdim

Six hun - dred three score and six And I will kill him one

ha ha ha ha ha ha ha ha ha ha ha ha

ha ha ha ha ha ha ha ha

44

G♯m Ddim E♭m Adim

day He's no great man ___ None of us are great men We're caught in the

ha ha ha ha ha ha ha ha ha ha ha ha

ha ha ha ha ha ha ha ha

46

B♭m Edim Fm Bdim

wave ___ of his - to - ry Noth-ing mat - ters Ev - ery - thing

ha ha ha ha ha ha ha ha ha ha ha ha

ha ha ha ha ha ha ha ha

48 Cm F♯dim Gm C♯dim

mat - ters It's all the same Oh if on - ly I could not see *it* This

ha ha ha ha ha ha ha ha ha ha ha ha

ha ha ha ha ha ha ha ha

50 Dm G♯dim Am

dread - ful, ter - ri - ble *it!*

ha ha ha ha ha In nine - teenth cen - tury Rus - sia we write

ha ha ha ha In nine - teenth cen - tury Rus - sia we write

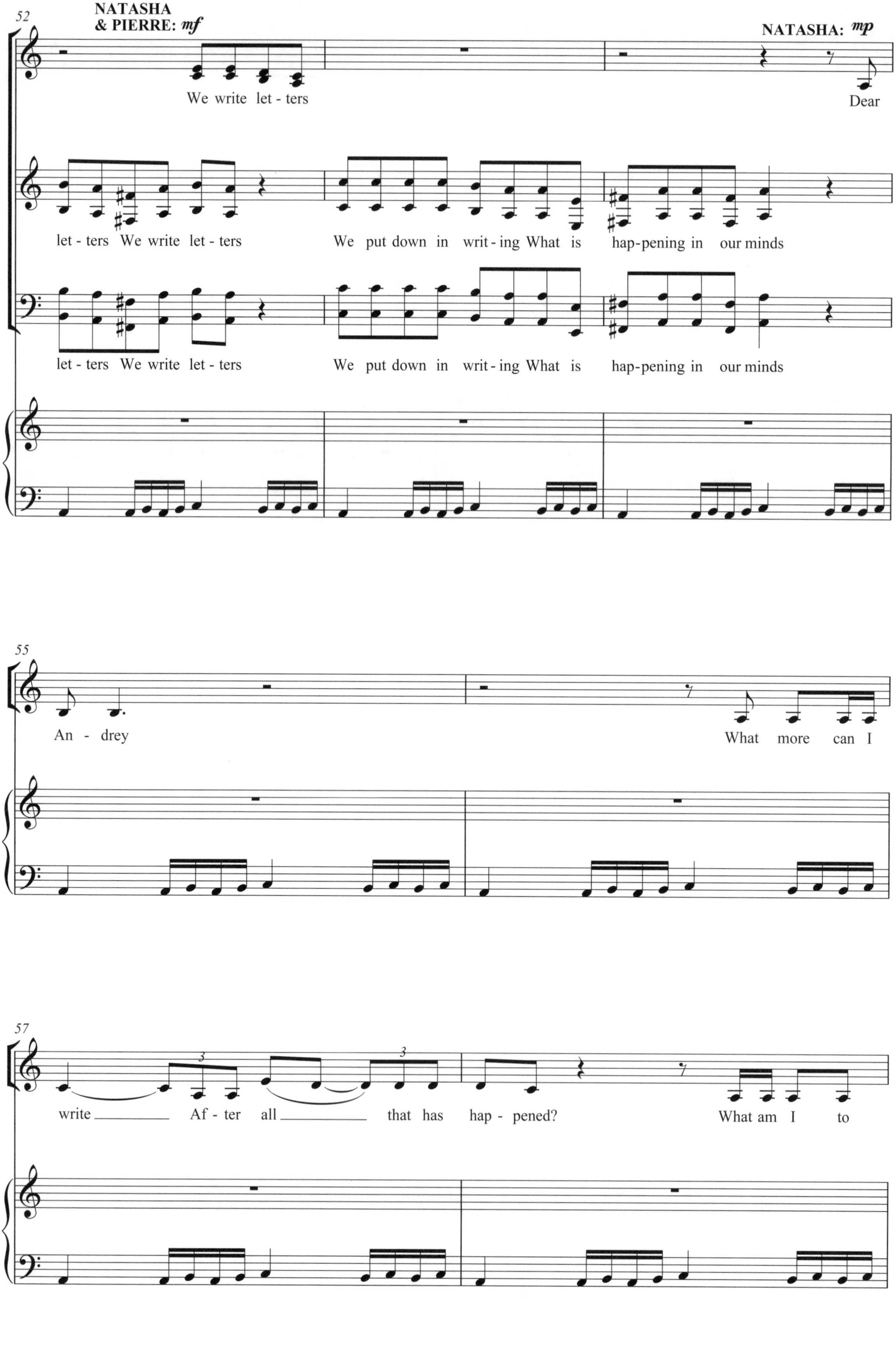

52

NATASHA & PIERRE: *mf*

NATASHA: *mp*

We write let - ters

Dear

let - ters We write let - ters We put down in writ - ing What is hap-pening in our minds

let - ters We write let - ters We put down in writ - ing What is hap-pening in our minds

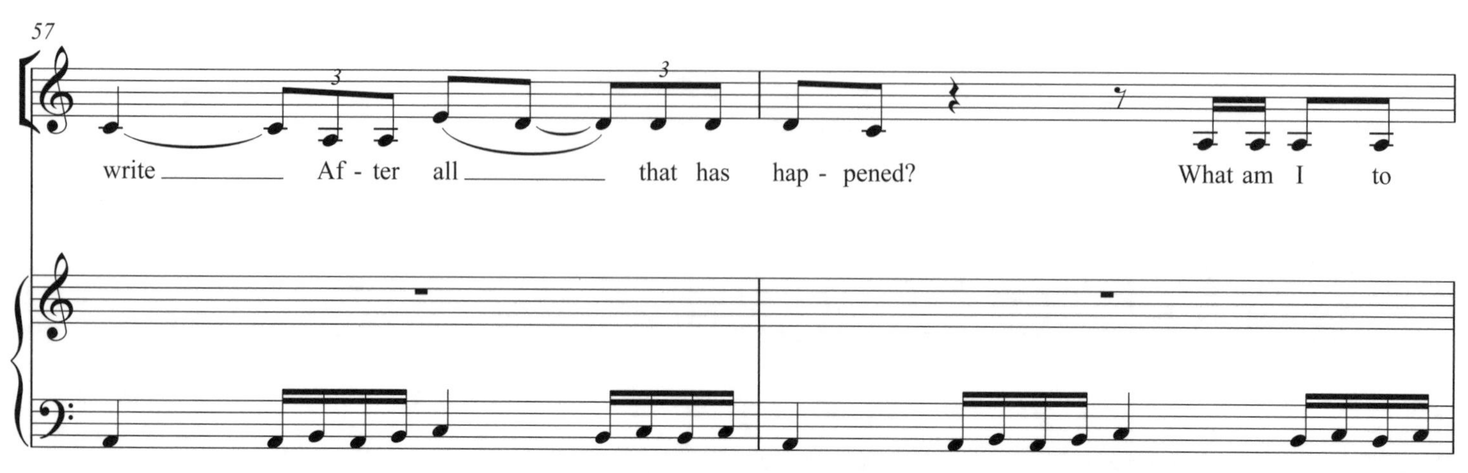

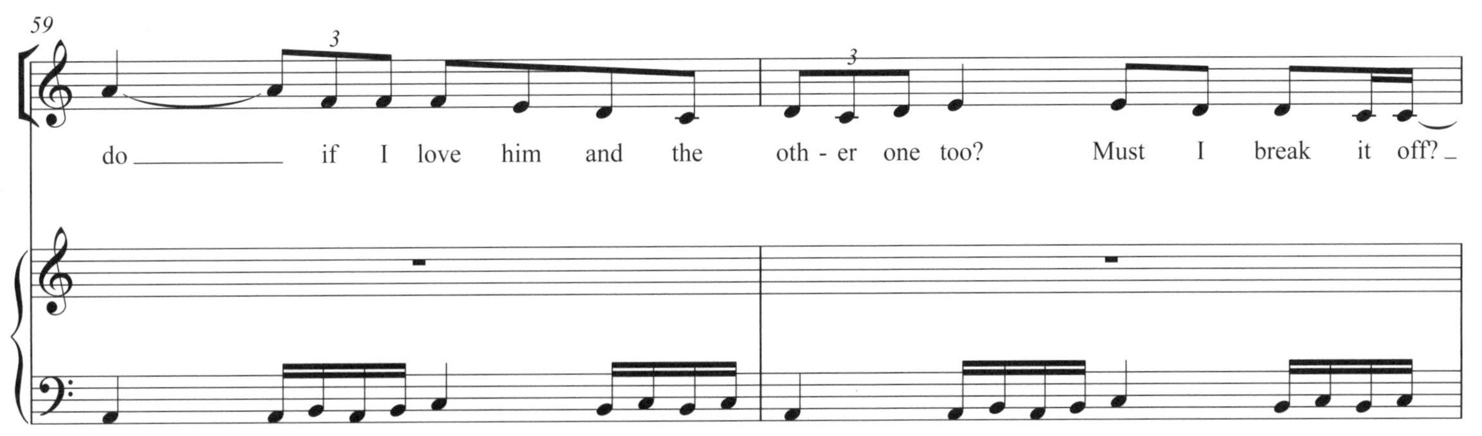
59
do ___ if I love him and the oth - er one too? Must I break it off? _

61
Dm
mf
__ These ter - ri - ble ques - tions I see
PIERRE: mf
I see

63
Am
noth-ing but the can - dle in the mirror _ No vi-sions of the fu -
noth-ing but the can - dle in the mirror _ No vi-sions of the fu -
mp

65
- ture So lost and a - lone And
- ture So lost and a - lone
67
Dm
MARY:
mp
what of Prin - cess Mar - y Dear Na - ta - sha
69
E7
Am
E7
I'm in deep des - pair at the mis - un - der - stand - ing there is be - tween us What -
Ha
Ha
Ha
Ha

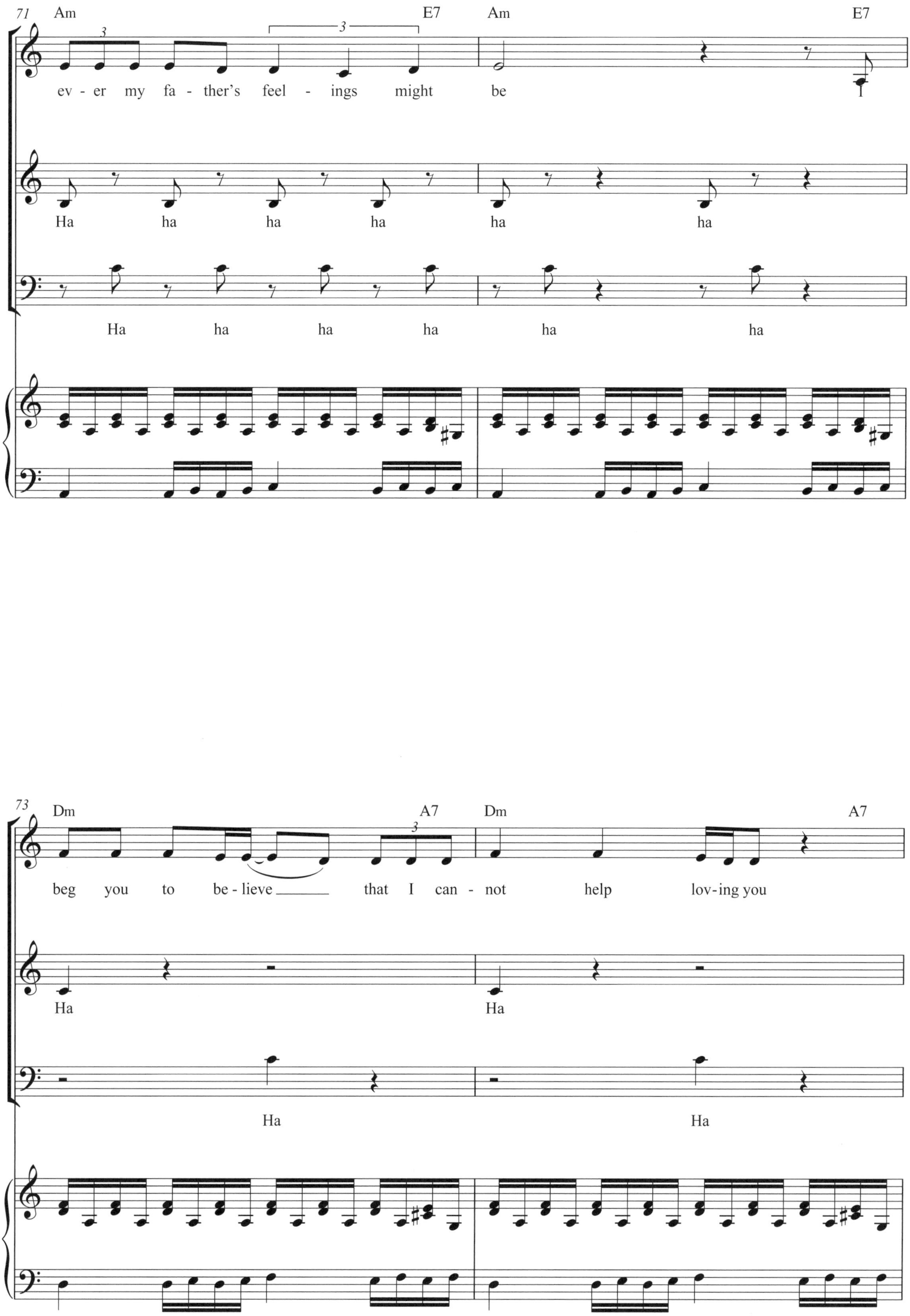

71 Am E7 Am E7

ev - er my fa - ther's feel - ings might be I

Ha ha ha ha ha ha

Ha ha ha ha ha ha

75
Am
E7
Am
E7
He is a ti - red old man and must be for - giv - en
Please, come
Ha ha ha ha ha ha
Ha ha ha ha ha ha

77
E7♭9
E7
E7♭9
f
see us a-gain
Prin - cess Mar - y
Oh
Ha
Ha
Ha
Ha

79
E7
E7♭9
E7
E7♭9
what am I to write! How do I choose What do I do I shall ne - ver be hap - py a - gain
PIERRE: f
These
Ha ha ha ha ha ha
Ha ha ha ha ha ha
81
Am
E♭dim
mf
Em
B♭dim
I'm so a - lone here
ter - ri - ble ques - tions
ha ha ha ha ha ha ha ha ha ha ha ha ha
ha ha ha ha ha ha ha ha

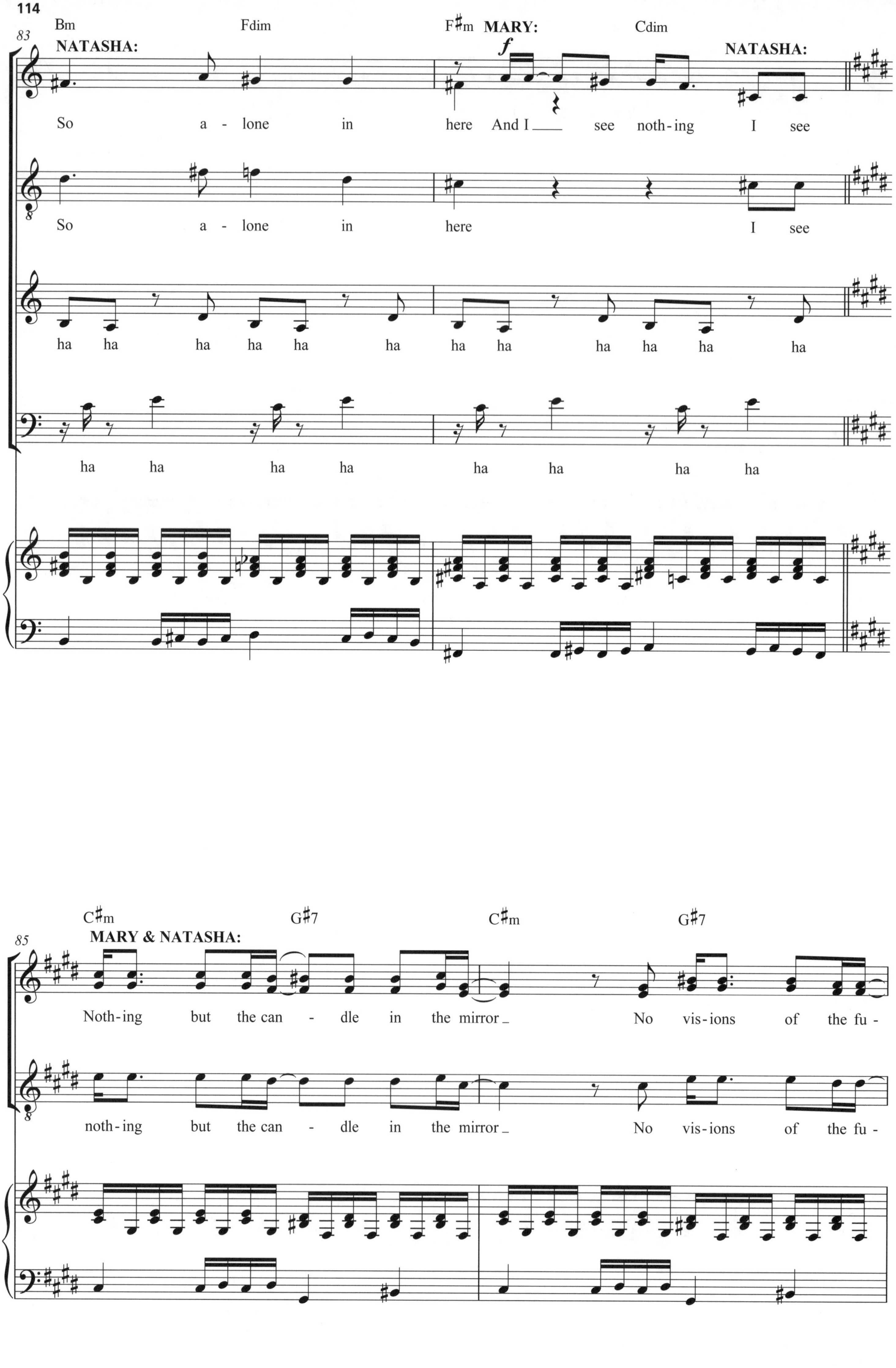

83

Bm Fdim F♯m Cdim

NATASHA: **MARY:** *f* **NATASHA:**

So a - lone in here And I ___ see noth-ing I see

So a - lone in here I see

ha ha ha ha ha ha ha ha ha ha ha ha

ha ha ha ha ha ha ha ha

87

C♯m G♯7 C♯m G♯dim7

- ture So lost and a - lone

- ture So lost and a - lone

CHORUS:
Whoa whoa whoa In

CHORUS:
In

89

Am E7 Am E7

NATASHA & PIERRE: *mf*
We write let - ters

MARY & ANATOLE:
We write let - ters

nine - teenth cen - tury Rus - sia we write let - ters We write let - ters

nine - teenth cen - tury Rus - sia we write let - ters We write let - ters

91
Am
E7
Am
ANATOLE: mp
E7
Dear
We put down in writ - ing What is hap - pening in our minds
We put down in writ - ing What is hap - pening in our minds

93
Am
Dm/A
G♯dim7/A
Nat - a - lie A love let - ter A love let - ter A

96
Am
NATASHA: mp
love let - ter A let - ter from him, from the man that I love
DOLOKHOV: mf
A

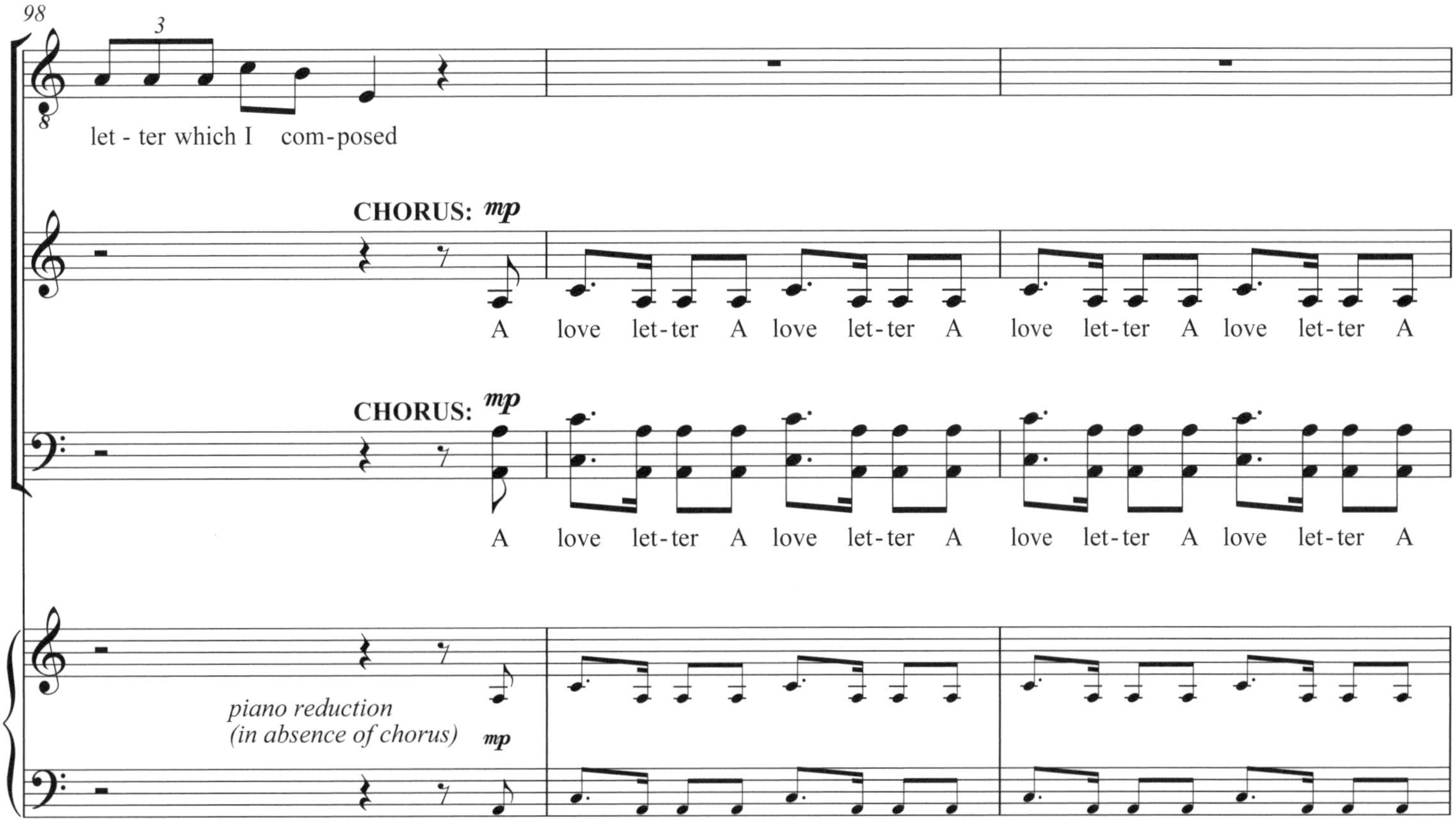

98
3
let - ter which I com-posed
CHORUS: mp
A love let-ter A love let-ter A love let-ter A love let-ter A
CHORUS: mp
A love let-ter A love let-ter A love let-ter A love let-ter A
piano reduction
(in absence of chorus)
mp

101
HÉLÈNE:
love let - ter A love let - ter A love let - ter A love let - ter A
love let - ter A love let - ter A love let - ter A love let - ter A

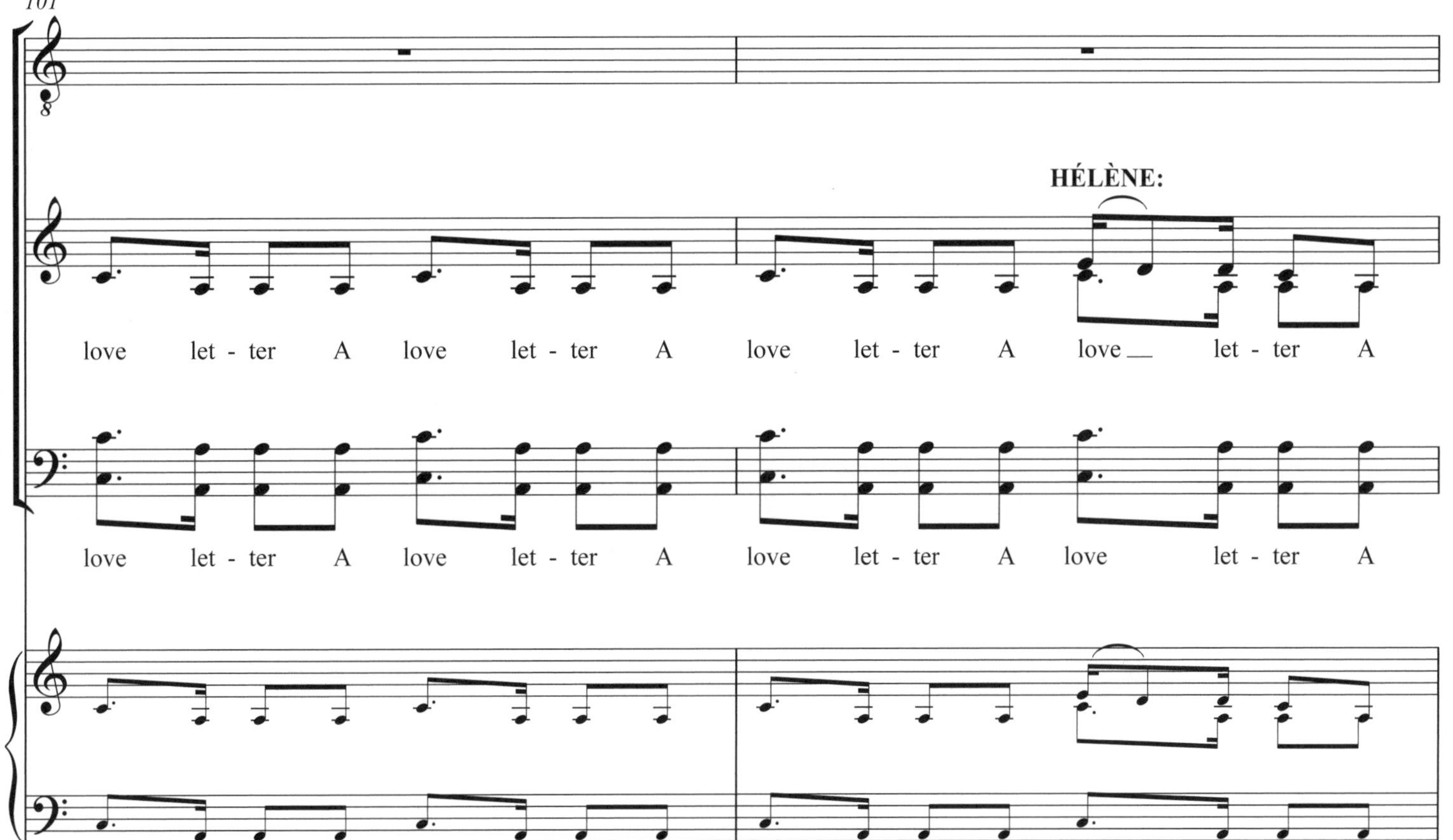

ANATOLE:

103

mf

Na - ta - lie Na - ta - lie Na - ta - lie I must love you or die

love let - ter A love let - ter A love let - ter A love let - ter A

love let - ter A love let - ter A love let - ter A love let - ter A

105

Na - ta - lie Na - ta - lie Na - ta - lie If you love me say yes And I will come

love let - ter A love let - ter A love let - ter A love let - ter A

love let - ter A love let - ter A love let - ter A love let - ter A

107

___ and steal you a - way Steal ___ you out of the dark

love let - ter A love let - ter A love let - ter A love _ let - ter A

love let - ter A love let - ter A love let - ter A love let - ter A

109

Na - ta - lie Na - ta - lie Na - ta - lie I want noth - ing more

love let - ter A love let - ter A love let - ter A love _ let - ter A

love let - ter A love let - ter A love let - ter A love let - ter A

111
f
Na - ta - lie Na - ta - lie Na - ta - lie I must love you or die
MARY, SONYA,
MARYA & PIERRE:
ff
Na - ta - lie Na - ta - lie Na - ta - lie
f
love let - ter A love let - ter A love let - ter A love let - ter A
f
love let - ter A love let - ter A love let - ter A love let - ter A
f
113
Na - ta - lie Na - ta - lie Na - ta - lie If you love me say yes And I will come
ff
belted
Na - ta - lie Na - ta - lie Na - ta - lie
love let - ter A love let - ter A love let - ter A love let - ter A
love let - ter A love let - ter A love let - ter A love let - ter A

115
ossia
and steal you a-way Steal you out of the dark
Huh Huh Huh Huh
love let-ter A love let-ter A love let-ter A love let-ter A
love let-ter A love let-ter A love let-ter A love let-ter A
117
mp
Na-ta-lie Na-ta-lie Na-ta-lie I want noth - ing more Just say yes Just say
Na-ta-lie Na-ta-lie Na-ta-lie
love let-ter A love let-ter A love let-ter A love let-ter
love let-ter A love let-ter A love let-ter A love let-ter

Moderately, in 1
120
p
3
falsetto
yes Just say yes
Dm
NATASHA:
mp
Yes,
B♭
yes, I
loco
124
F
love him!
A7/C♯
How else could I
Dm
have his
B♭
4
let - ter in my
128
F
hand?
I read it
C7
twen - ty times
132
C♯dim7
Thir - ty times, for - ty times!
Dm
Each and
C
ev - ery

136
B♭
C7
word
I
love
him,
I
140
2
A7
love
him
144
Dm7
B♭
F
mp
149
A7/C♯
Dm
Dm/C
B♭7
molto rit.
attacca

SONYA & NATASHA

Music and Lyrics by
DAVE MALLOY
Based on *War and Peace* by Leo Tolstoy

Moderately

10
E♭
B♭7
back And ___ with the ten - der re - solve that of - ten comes at the
12
B♭7♭9
E♭
Bdim7
A♭dim7
mo-ment of a-wak-en-ing I em-braced my friend But no-tic-ing Son-ya's
15
Fdim7
Ddim7
Bdim7
Cm
Adim7
look of em-bar-rass-ment My face ex-pressed con - fu - sion And sus -
18
Gm
E♭dim7
G♭dim7
Adim7
Cdim7
E♭dim7
SONYA:
NATASHA:
pi-cion Son-ya, you've read the let-ter? Yes Oh Son-ya, I'm

20
E♭
B♭
A7
glad I can't hide it an - y long - er! Now you know, we love one an -
23
Dm
Dm/C
B♭
2
oth - er! Oh Son - ya, he writes, he writes He writes, he writes, he
26
A7
SONYA: mf
Dm/A
NATASHA: mf
writes And An - drey? Oh Son - ya, if you on - ly knew how hap - py I
mf
29
3
SONYA:
am! You don't know what love is But Na - ta - sha, can that all be

32
A7
NATASHA:
SONYA:
Dm
B♭
NATASHA:
o - ver? I do not grasp the quest - ion Are you re - fu - sing Prince An - drey? Oh,
35
E♭
B♭
G7
Cm
Cm/B♭
SONYA:
you don't un - der - stand an - y - thing! Don't talk non - sense, just lis - ten But I
f
37
A♭
E♭
G7
Cm
G7
A♭
E♭
can't be - lieve it, I don't un - der - stand How you loved one man a whole year and
39
Edim7
Fm
Fm6
Fm(maj7)
Fm
sud - den - ly You've on - ly known him three days! Na - ta - sha, you're jok - ing!

Slower
41
A♭ G Gm/G♯
NATASHA:
mp
Three days? It seems to me I've loved him a hun-dred
p
44
Am G♯dim7
rit.
years It seems to me I've nev-er loved an-y-one be-
rit.
46
Am C/G F E/F F Fm(maj7) Fm6
fore Not like this I have no
Brightly (♩ = 𝅗𝅥.)
49
Am/E Fm6 Am/E
will My life is his

54
mf
B7
Em
I'll do an - y - thing he wants me to
mf
58
Am6
Em
Am6
Em
f
What can I do? Son - ya, what can I do? I'm
Fast, in 1
63
C
G
so happ - py
f
68
B7
And so

73 Em | C | G/B

fright - ened Why can't you un - der - stand?

78 F/A | SONYA: | Am7♭5

I love him! Then I won't let it come to

83

that, I ___ shall tell! Burst - ing

88 G | G7/F

in - to tears ___

f

93
G7/E♭
G7/D
NATASHA:
ff
3
What do you
A little fiercer
97
Bm
F♯7
Bm
F♯7
4
mean? For God's sake, if you tell, you are my en - e - my! You
ff
101
Bm
F♯7
Bm
F♯7
4
3
want me to be mis - 'ra - ble You want to tear us a - part For
105
Bm
F♯7
Bm
F♯7
4
God's sake, Son - ya, don't tell an - y - one, don't tor - ture me

109
SONYA: f
Em
I have con - fid - ed in you
What has
mf
114
D
Em
D
hap - pened be - tween you? What has he said to you?
119
C♯7
C♯7/E♯
F♯m
G
Why does - n't he come to the house and o - pen - ly ask for your
124
D
B7♭9
hand? Why this se - cre -

129
Am
G
F#7
NATASHA:
cy? Have you thought what his se - cret rea - sons may be? I don't
134
B7♭9
know what the rea - sons are But there must be rea - sons!
f
138
Am
B7
SONYA:
mp
Sweetly, in time
Son - ya, one can't doubt him! Does he love you?
mp
143
NATASHA:
mp
G/B
F#7/A#
Does he love me? Why, you've read his let - ter, you've

148
Bm
F♯7/A♯
Bm
SONYA:
seen him I can't live with - out him Na -

153
G
B7
Em
ta - sha, think of our fam - ily And think of Prince An - drey
mf

158
NATASHA:
E7/G♯
Am
SONYA:
An - drey said I was free to re - fuse him But you

163
Dm
Bdim7
G♯dim7
NATASHA:
E7
Am
hav - en't re - fused him, or have you? Per - haps I have
mp

168
F
dolcissimo
C
Per - haps all is o - ver be - tween me and Bol - kon - sky
p
173
F
Fm6
C
Would you think so bad - ly of me?
With gusto
178
SONYA:
G7
f
I won't suc-cumb to your ten - der tone Na - ta - sha I don't trust him, Na - ta - sha! I'm a -
181
Cm
A♭
E♭
G7
ff
NATASHA:
fraid for you, Na - ta - sha! A - fraid you are go - ing to your ru - in Then I'll go to my

184
Cm Ab Eb G7 Cm Cm/Eb Fm Eb/Bb Db C7
ru - in, yes I will, as soon as pos-si-ble! But it's not your bus-iness! It won't be you, it-'ll be
187
Fm Abdim Bdim7 C7b9
ff
me, who'll suf - fer Leave me a - lone, yes leave me a - lone! I
189
G7b9(#11)
hate you, Son - ya! I hate you, Son - ya! I hate you, I hate you! You're my
192
Slower, stately
SONYA:
ff
Eb Db C7
molto rall.
en - e - my for - ev - er! I burst in - to sobs
ff
rit.

Slowly
NATASHA:
195
Fm11
f
And with - out a mo - ment's re - flec - tion I wrote the an - swer to Prin - cess
197
Mar - y I'd been un - a - ble to write all morn - ing
199
D♭
A♭
G7
All our mis - un - der - stand - ings are at an end For - get ev - ery - thing and for -
mf colla voce
201
Cm
C7/B♭
Fm/A♭
Fm
molto rit.
give me But I can't be An - drey's wife
molto rit.

SONYA ALONE

Music and Lyrics by
DAVE MALLOY
Based on *War and Peace* by Leo Tolstoy

13
Em7
Gm6
D A Bm F♯
waits by the win - dow And I lis - ten at the door Un - til one day I see by the
16
G D
D A Bm F♯
G D
sad look on her face There is a dread - ful plan in her heart
19
Bm D/A
G D
Bm D/A
I know you are cap - a - ble of an - y - thing I know you so
22
G D
Bm D/A
G D
mf
well my friend I know you might just run a - way What am I to
mf

25
Em7
mp
3
3
Gm6
3
do? Who do I ask for help? Is it all on me? Is it all on
mp
28
Gm(maj7) Gm6 D A Bm F♯
3
G D
me? Oh I will stand in the dark for you
mf
31
D A Bm F♯ G D D A Bm F♯
I will hold you back by force I will stand here
3
34
G D D A Bm F♯ G D
right out-side your door I won't see you dis-graced
3

Em7
Gm6
D A Bm F♯
37
I will pro - tect your name and your heart Be - cause I miss my friend
G D
D A Bm F♯
G D
Bm D/A
40
p
I know you've for -
pp
G
Bm D/A
G D
Bm D/A
44
mf
got - ten me I know you so well my friend I know you might just
poco più mosso
G D
Em7
48
throw your - self o - ver But I won't let you I won't let you It's all on

51
Gm(maj7)
Gm6
G
f
me
And I re - mem - ber this fam - ily I re -
54
F♯
F♯7/A♯
Bm
D/A
G
mem - ber their kind - ness And if I nev - er sleep a - gain
ff
mf
57
D A Bm F♯ G D D A Bm F♯
I will stand in the dark for you
I will hold you
60
G D D A Bm F♯ G D
back by force
I will stand here right out - side your door

63
D A Bm F♯ G D Em7
mf
I won't see you dis - graced I will pro - tect your
mp
3
66
Gm6 D A Bm F♯ G D
mp
name and your heart Be - cause I miss my friend Be -
mp
69
D A Bm F♯ G D D A Bm F♯
cause I miss my friend Be - cause I miss you, my
p
3
72
G D D A Bm F♯ G D
friend

BALAGA

Music and Lyrics by
DAVE MALLOY
Based on *War and Peace* by Leo Tolstoy

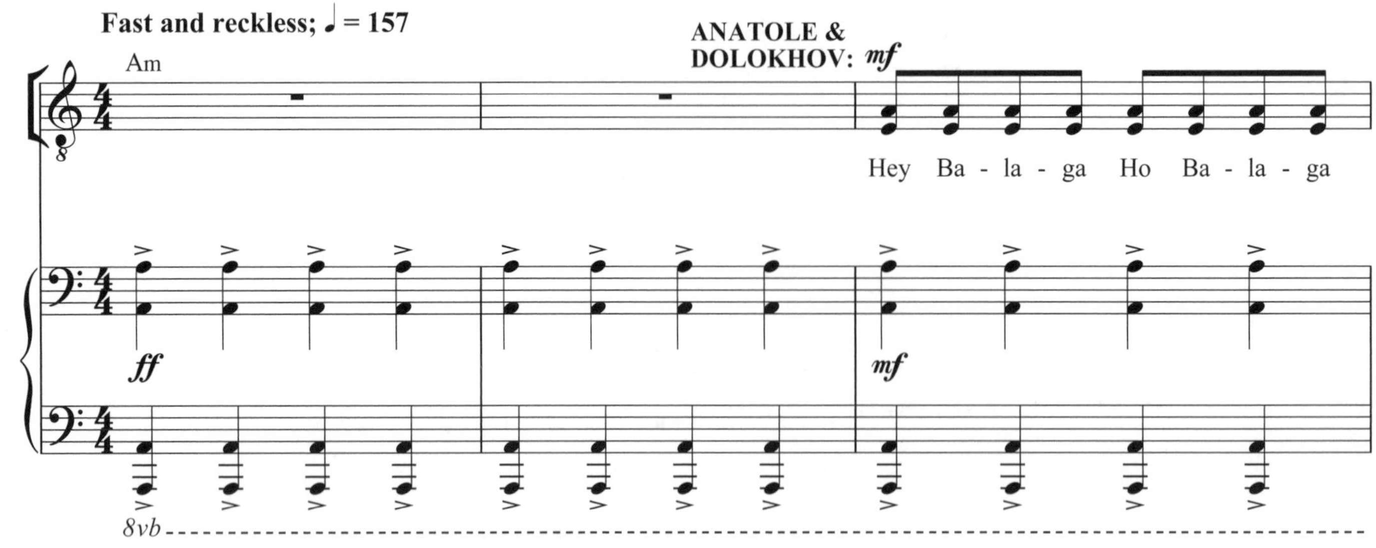

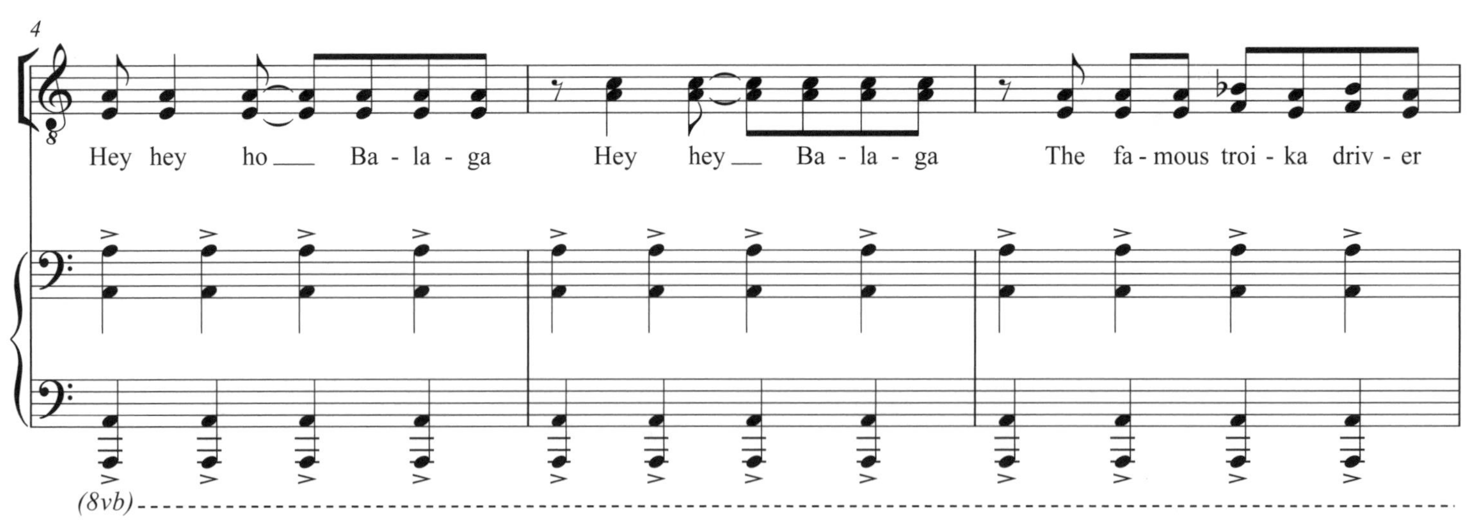

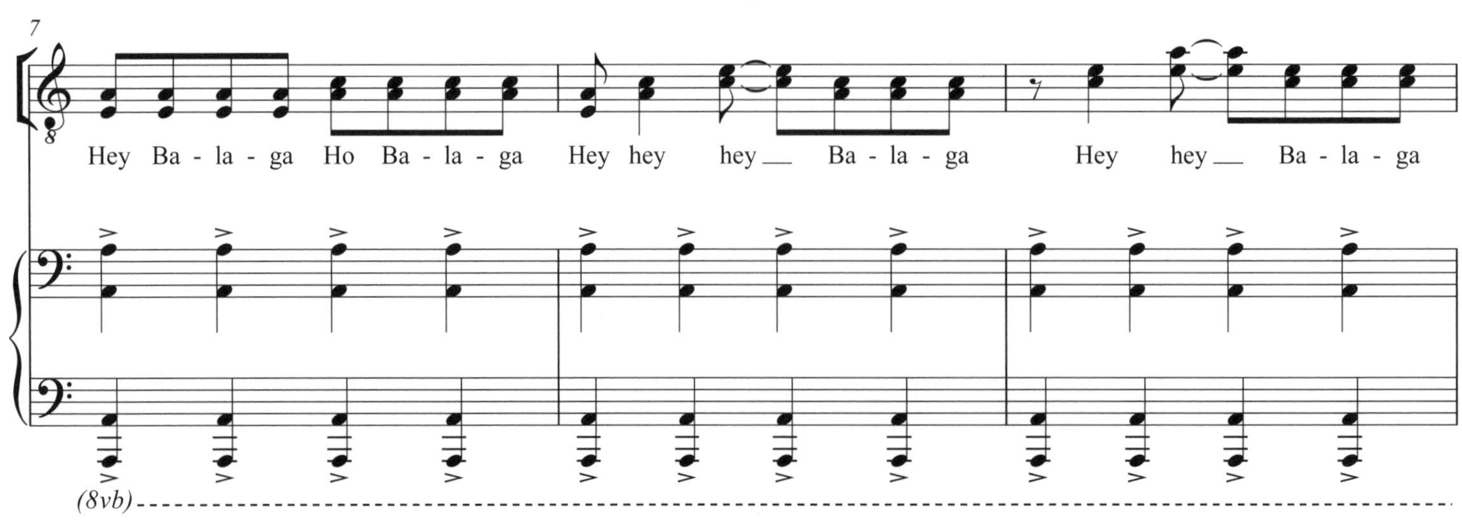

10
Dm
BALAGA:
The fa-mous troi-ka driv-er
Who's that mad-man fly-ing at full gal-lop down the
(8vb)
13
Am
street
Dm
Who's that mad-man
16
knock-ing peo-ple o-ver Run-ning peo-ple down
While his fine gen-tle-men
18
E7
Hold on to their seats
ANATOLE & DOLOKHOV: f
It's Ba-
8vb

21 Am Dm Am Dm Am Dm

Driv-ing mad at twelve miles an hour Com-ing straight at you Get

la - ga! Ba - la - ga!

f

24 Am Dm Am Dm Am Dm

out my way, get out my way Lash-in' my whip at hors - es and pea-sants

Ba - la - ga! Ba -

27 Am Dm Am Am7

Risk-ing skin and life twen-ty times a year For my fine fine gen - tle - men

la - ga!

30
Am
Yes sir hey ho yes sir
Yes sir yes sir yes sir
More than
33
E7
B♭7
E7
From Tu-la to Mos cow and back in just one night
A nar-row es-cape from a
once!
More than once!
mf
cresc.
8vb
36
B♭7
E7
B♭7
wild Cos-sack fight
They've beat-en me and slapped me with their gloves
More than once!
More than
(8vb)

39 E7 Am

Made me drunk on cham - pagne, which I love!

once! Hey Ba - la - ga Ho Ba - la - ga

ALL: *f* Hey Ba - la - ga Ho Ba - la - ga

ALL: *f* Hey Ba - la - ga Ho Ba - la - ga

(8vb) *mf* 8vb

42

Hey hey ho Ba - la - ga Hey hey Ba - la - ga The fa - mous troi - ka driv - er

Hey hey ho Ba - la - ga Hey hey Ba - la - ga The fa - mous troi - ka driv - er

Hey hey ho Ba - la - ga Hey hey Ba - la - ga The fa - mous troi - ka driv - er

(8vb)

45

Hey Ba - la - ga Ho Ba - la - ga Hey hey hey __ Ba - la - ga Hey hey __ Ba - la - ga

Hey Ba - la - ga Ho Ba - la - ga Hey hey hey __ Ba - la - ga Hey hey __ Ba - la - ga

Hey Ba - la - ga Ho Ba - la - ga Hey hey hey __ Ba - la - ga Hey hey __ Ba - la - ga

(8vb)

48

Dm

ANATOLE:

The fa - mous troi - ka driv - er Who's that slow - poke we a - buse with wi - ld and tip - sy

3

The fa - mous troi - ka driv - er

The fa - mous troi - ka driv - er

(8vb)

51
Am
Dm6
BALAGA:
Who knows things that would
shouts?
54
get you sent straight to Si - ber - ia If an - y - one found
57
E7
Am
Dm
out
Driv - ing mad at
ANATOLE & DOLOKHOV:
It's Ba - la - ga!
CHORUS:
It's Ba - la - ga!
CHORUS:
It's Ba - la - ga!
f
8vb

60 Am Dm Am Dm

twelve miles an hour Com - ing straight at you Get

Ba - la - ga!

Ba - la - ga!

Ba - la - ga!

62 Am Dm Am Dm

out my way, get out my way Drink - ing and danc - ing with my

Ba - la - ga!

Ba - la - ga!

Ba - la - ga!

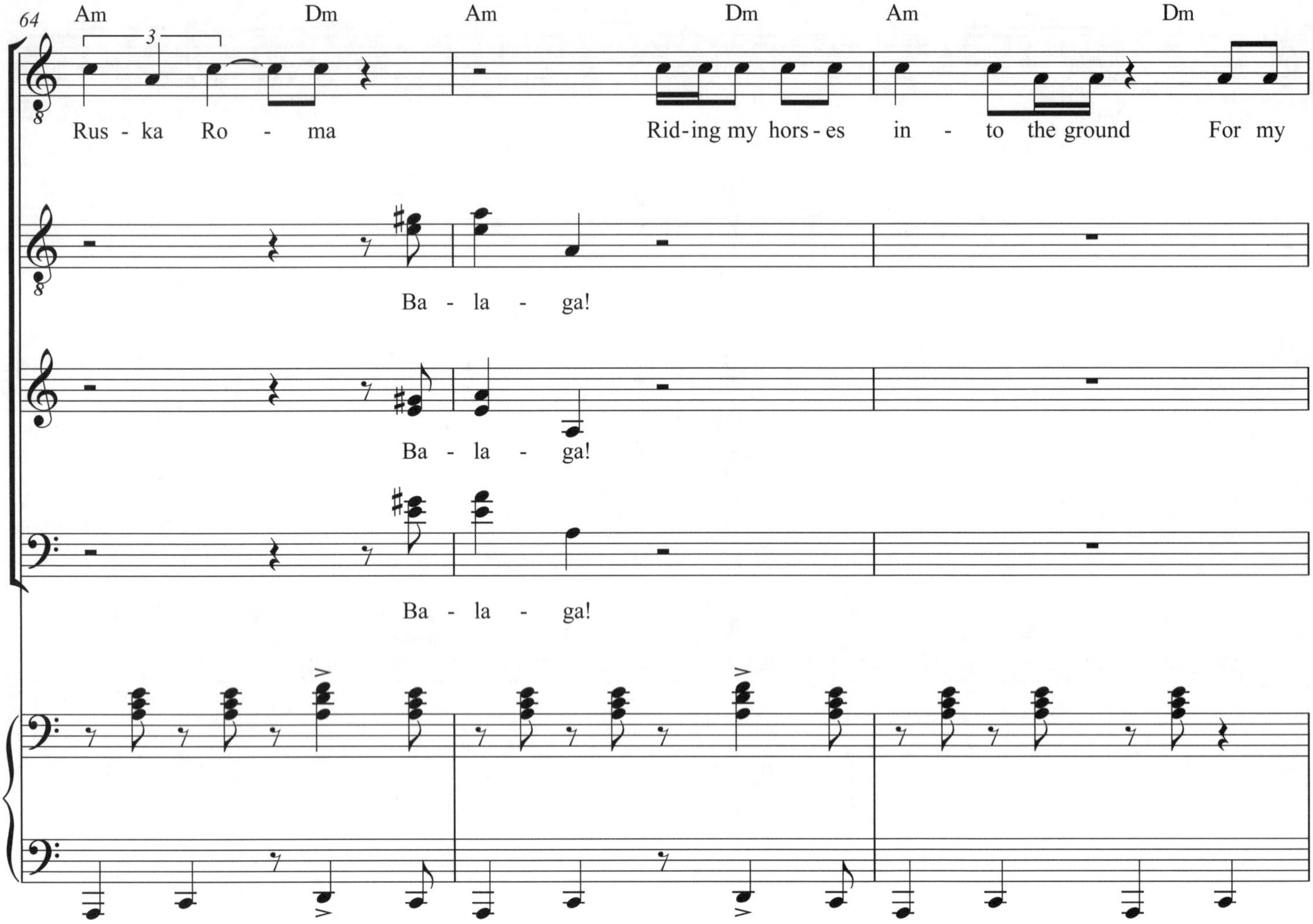

64

Am Dm Am Dm Am Dm

Rus - ka Ro - ma Rid-ing my hors-es in - to the ground For my

Ba - la - ga!

Ba - la - ga!

Ba - la - ga!

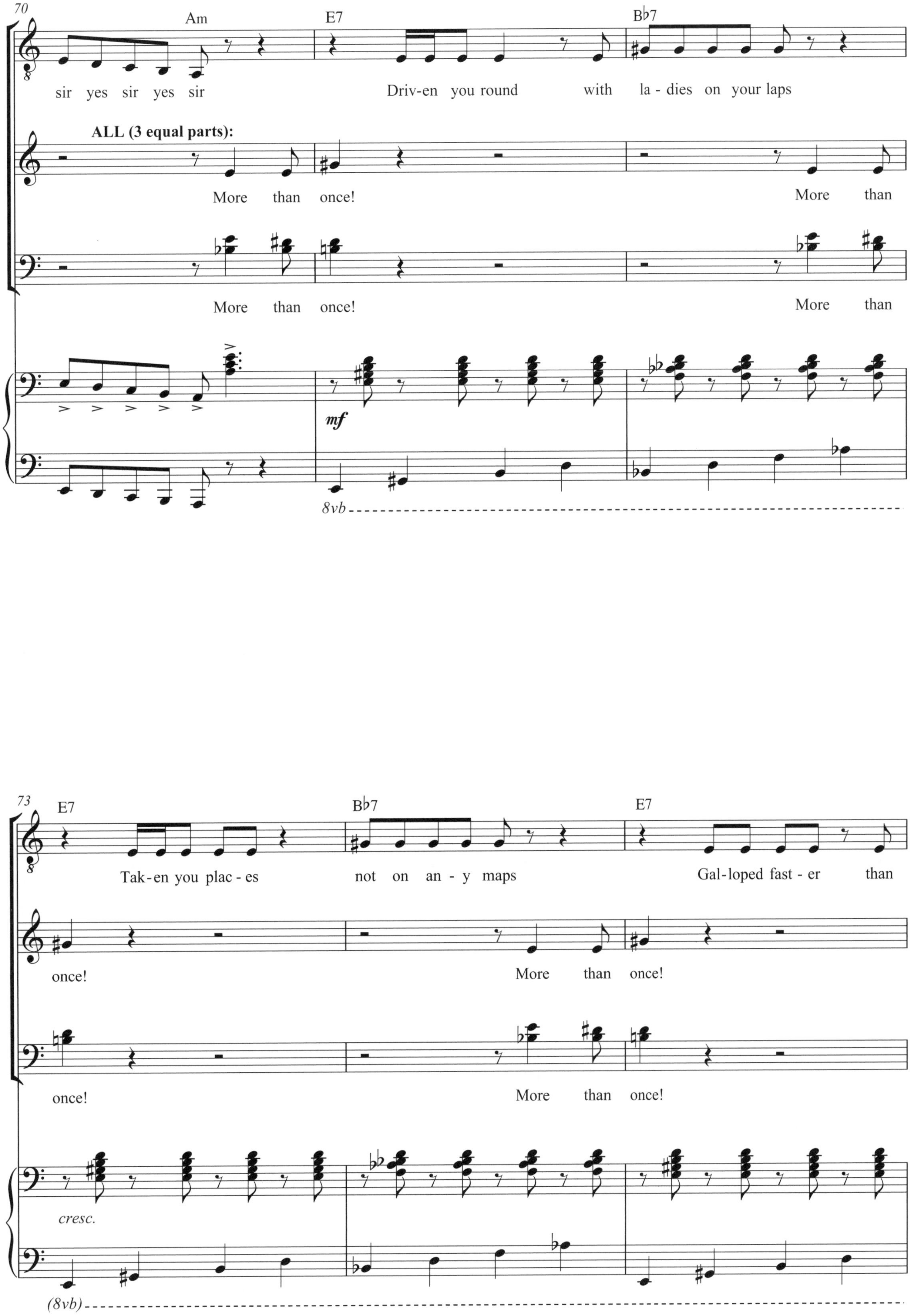

70

Am E7 B♭7

sir yes sir yes sir Driv-en you round with la - dies on your laps

ALL (3 equal parts):

More than once! More than

More than once! More than

mf

8vb

76
B♭7
E7
or - di - nar - y men would dare
Jumped my troi - ka right
in - to the air
More than once!
More than once!
(8vb)

79
A little slower
F
And I
nev - er ask for
f

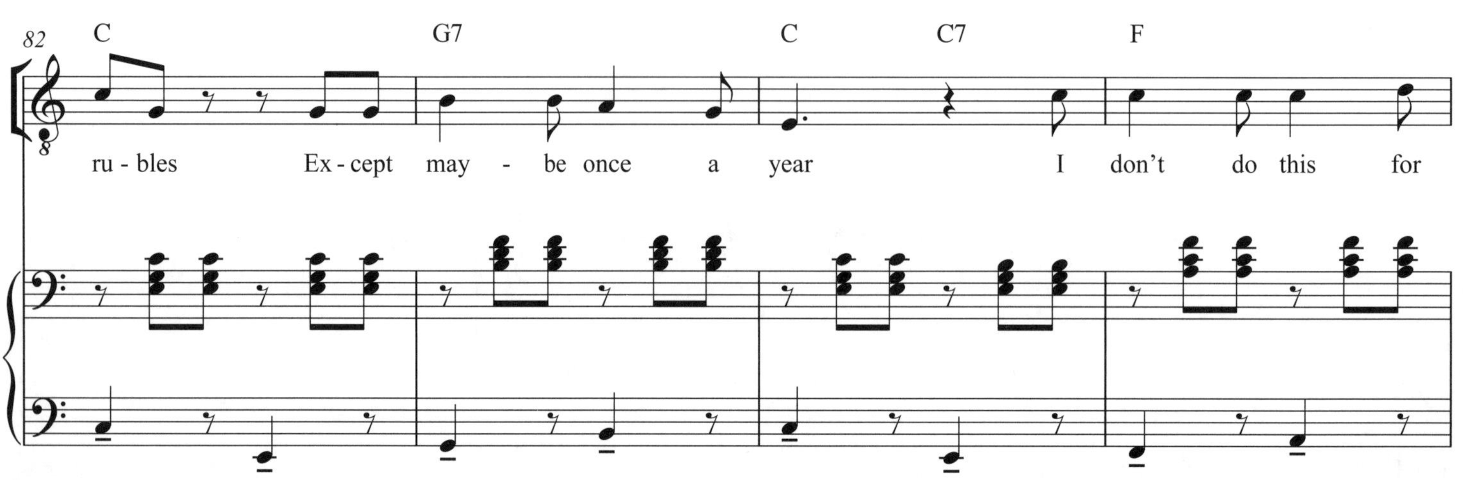
82
C
G7
C
C7
F
ru - bles
Ex - cept
may - be once a
year
I don't do this for

86
A tempo
C
E7
Am
ru - bles I do it cuz I like 'em!
ANATOLE & DOLOKHOV:
And we like Ba - la - ga too!
CHORUS:
And we like Ba - la - ga too!
CHORUS:
And we like Ba - la - ga too!
ANATOLE:
89
f
Whoa
Hit piano top (horse hooves)
f
92
ALL: ff
Whoa
ff
ALL:
Whoa
f
Stomp left foot

95

Dm

Whoa

Whoa

ff

98

Am

E7

Am

8vb

101

Dm

Am

E7

Am

Whoa

Whoa

8vb

attacca

THE ABDUCTION

Music and Lyrics by
DAVE MALLOY
Based on *War and Peace* by Leo Tolstoy

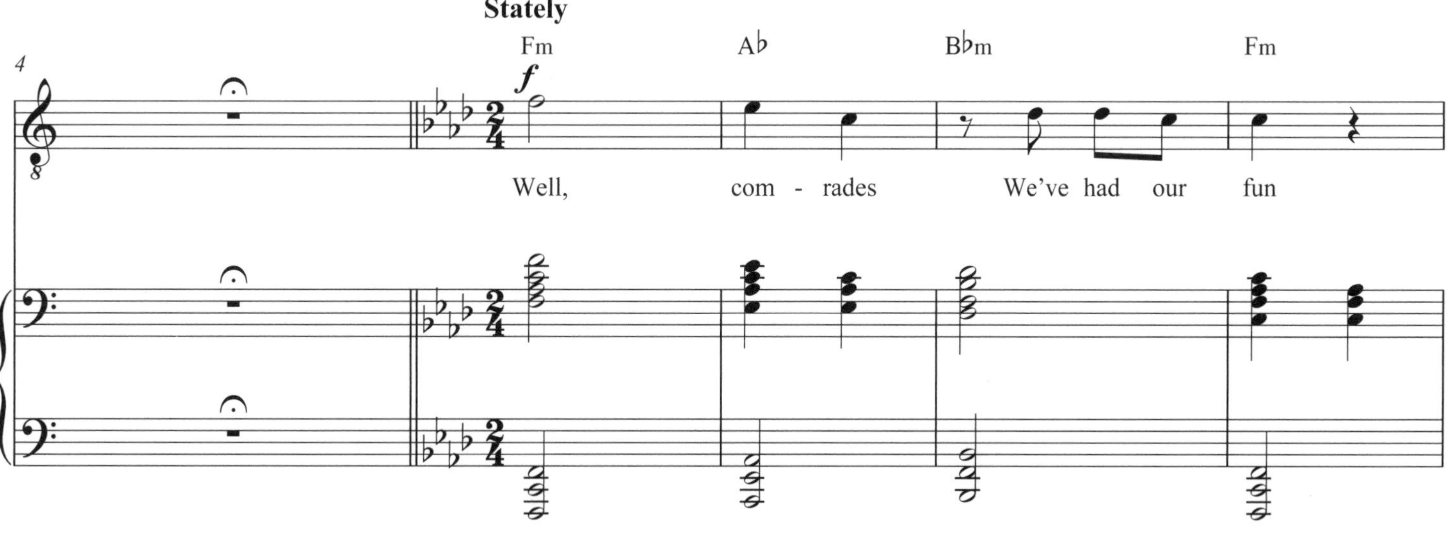

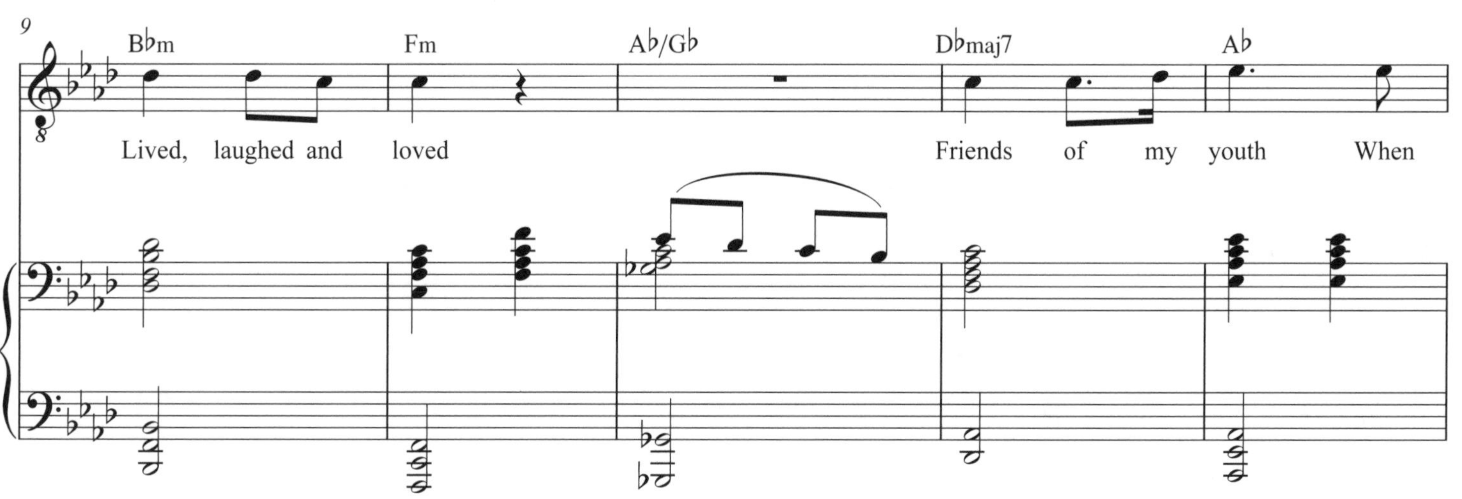

14
D♭m/A♭
A♭
G♭7
3
F7
F7/A
mf
shall we meet a - gain? I'm go - ing a - broad Good -
Stately Gypsy waltz
19
B♭m
bye my Gyp - sy lov - ers All my rev - els
mf
24
E♭m
here are o - ver Well, good - bye, Ma - try - o - sha
29
B♭m
Kiss me one last time, whoa

(harmony 2nd time only)
34
G♭
D♭
Re - mem - ber me to Stesh - ka There, good-
39
A♭/C
G♭
bye, good - bye, good - bye Wish me
43
G♭maj7
D♭
luck my Gyp - sy lov - ers Now good -
47
F7
B♭m
(2nd time ALL, BASSES 8vb)
bye, good - bye, good bye Good

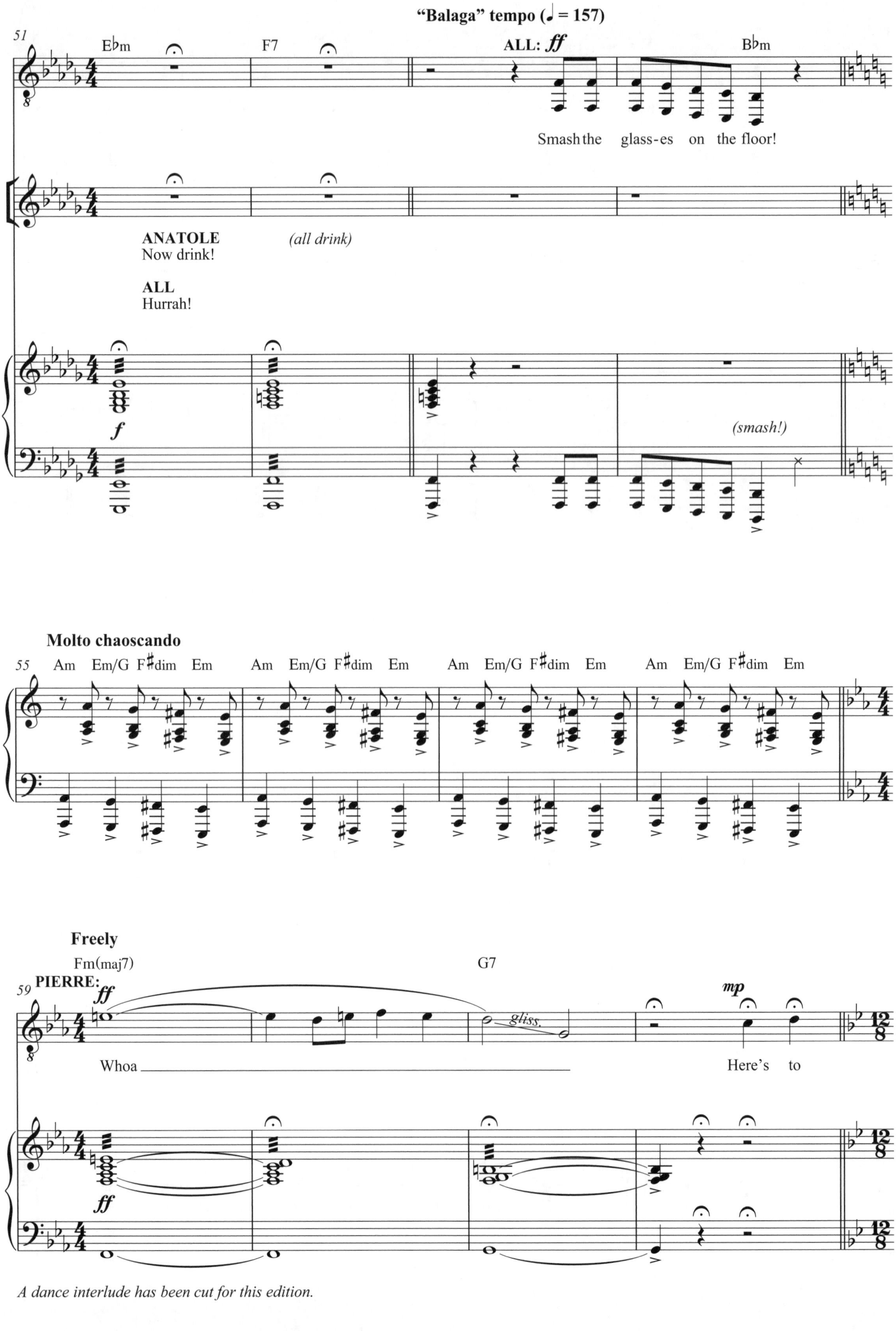

"Balaga" tempo (♩ = 157)

51 E♭m F7 ALL: *ff* B♭m

Smash the glass-es on the floor!

ANATOLE
Now drink!

(all drink)

ALL
Hurrah!

f

(smash!)

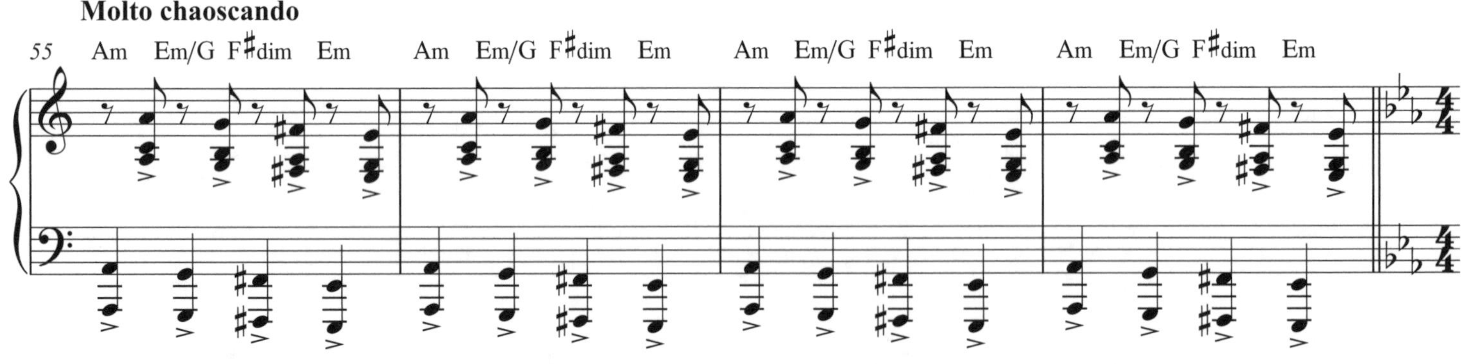

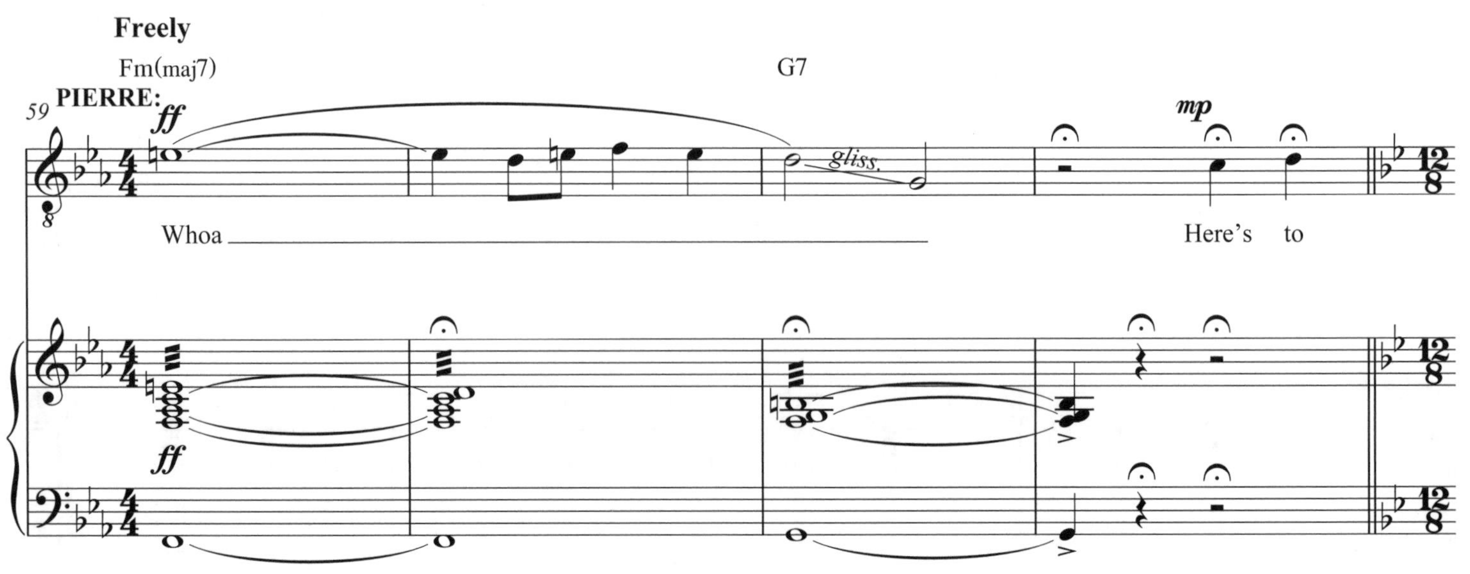

A dance interlude has been cut for this edition.

Jaunty (♩. = 140)
Cm
mf
hap - pi - ness, free - dom, and life!
May your
f
trav - el be swift as a scythe cuts through the grass!
Gm
CHORUS: mf
Whoa
CHORUS: mf
Whoa
Whoa
Whoa
Cm
May your sorr - ows be count - ed and num - ber as ma - ny As

69
Gm
drops of wine and vod - ka that stay in my glass!
Whoa
Whoa

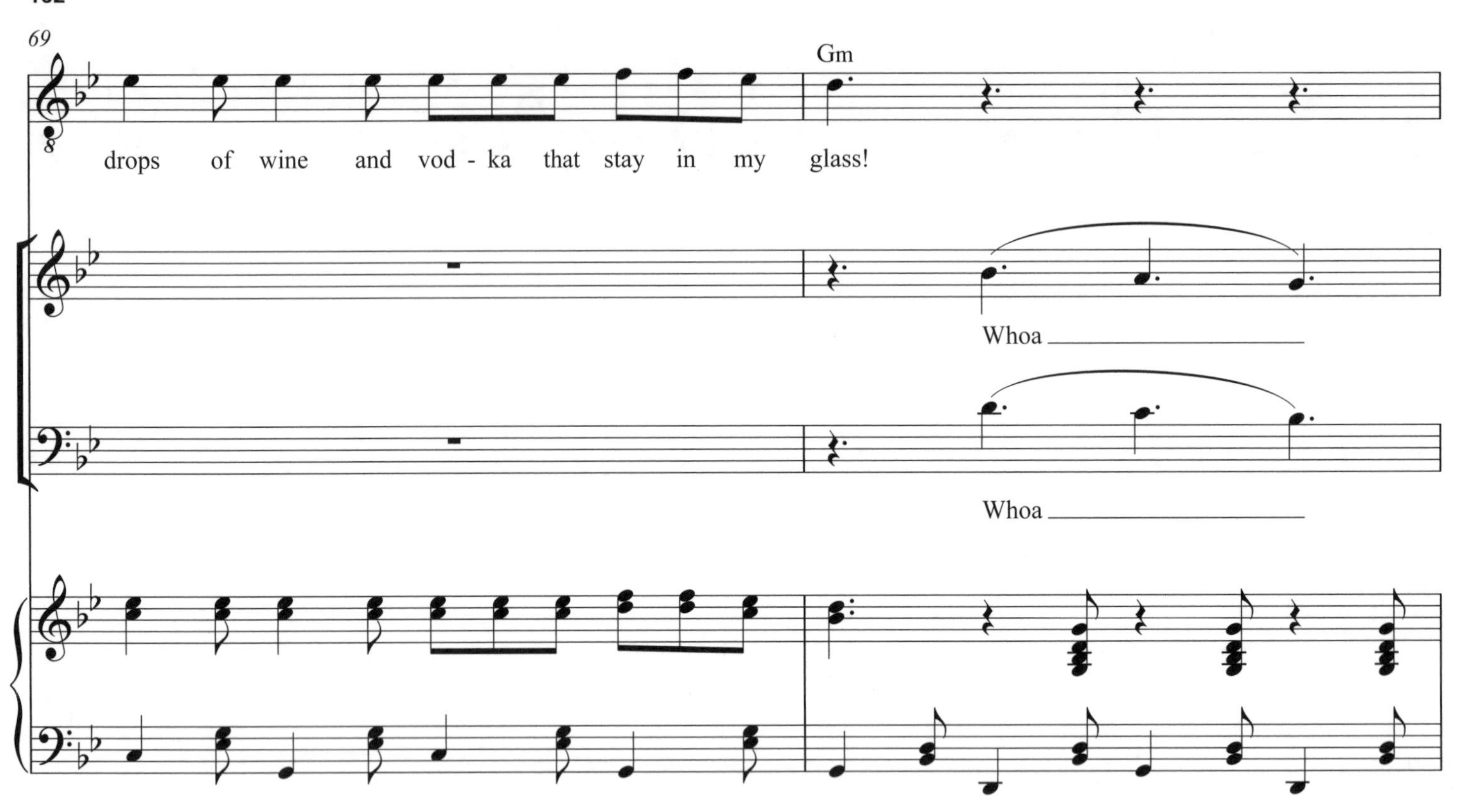

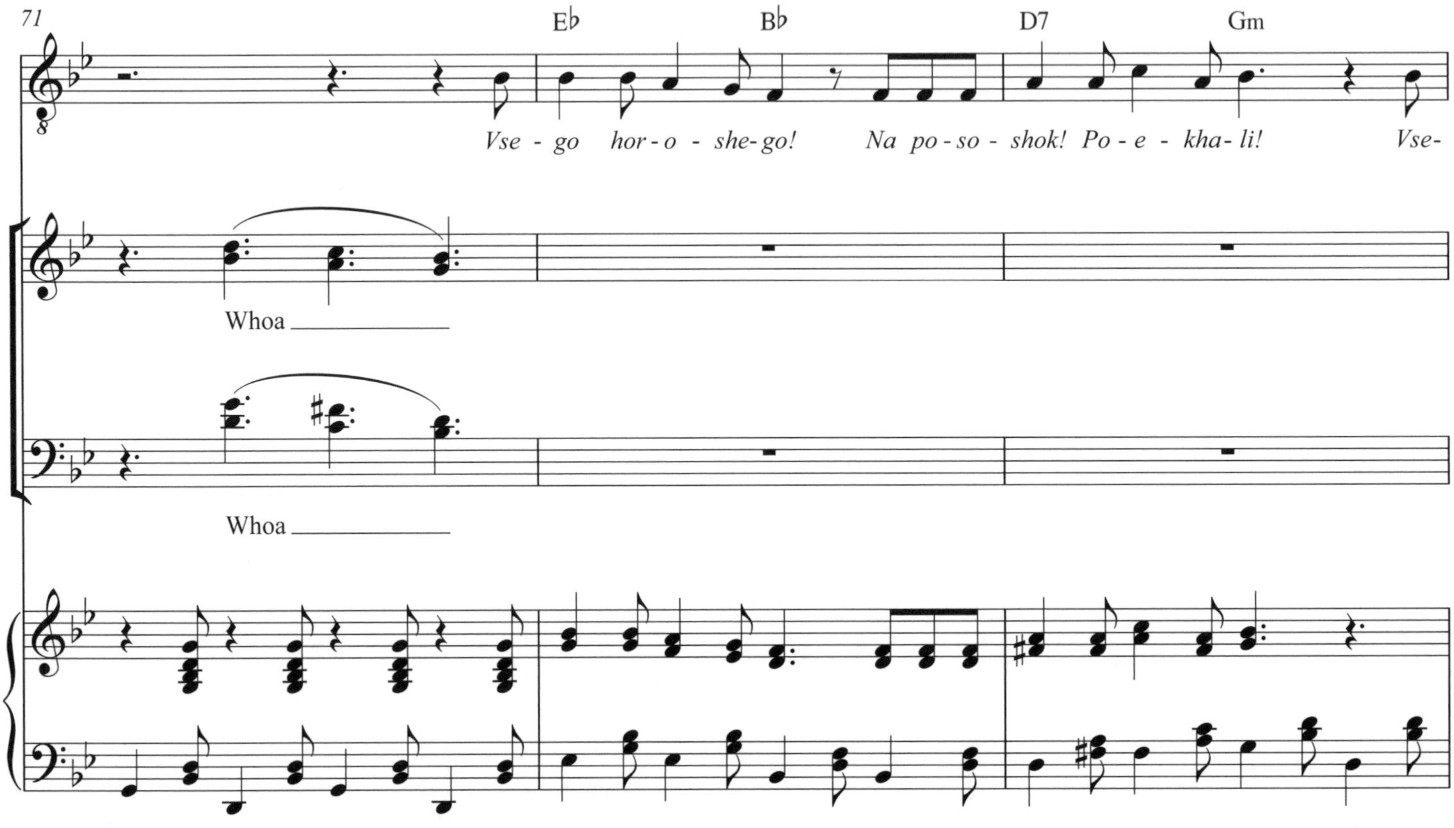

71
E♭ B♭ D7 Gm
Vse - go hor - o - she - go! Na po - so - shok! Po - e - kha - li! Vse-
Whoa
Whoa

74
E♭ B♭ D7 Gm E♭ B♭
go hor-o-she go! Na po-so-shok! Po-e-kha-li!
f
Vse-go hor-o-she go!
f
Na po-so-
77
D7 Gm E♭ B♭ D7
Vse-go hor-o-she-go! Po-e-kha-
shok! Po-e-kha-li! Na po-so-shok! Po-e-kha-
80
Gm D7 Gm D7 Gm
ff
li! Na po-so-shok! Po-e-kha-li!
li! Na po-so-shok! Po-e-kha-li!
ff

"Balaga" tempo (♩ = 157)
E♭m
B♭m
F7
B♭m
REPEAT AD LIB
until ANATOLE cuts off...
ALL: Come on!
Let's go, let's go!...
ANATOLE:
(door slam)
No, wait! Shut the door! First we have to sit down! That's the
way It's a Rus - sian cus - tom
lunga
lunga
All right!
E♭m
B♭m
DOLOKHOV:
Wait, wait, wait,
ALL: Come on!
Let's go, let's go!...

Bright waltz
96
Dm
mf
wait!
Where's the fur cloak?
mp

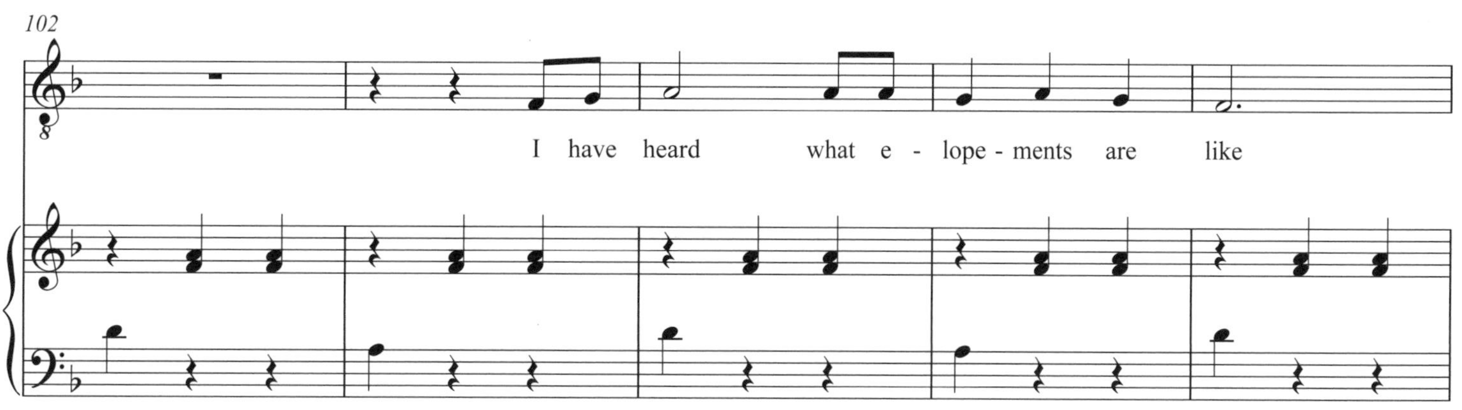
102
I have heard what e - lope - ments are like

107
She'll rush out more dead than a - live

112
Gm
Just in the things she's wear - ing If you de - lay at

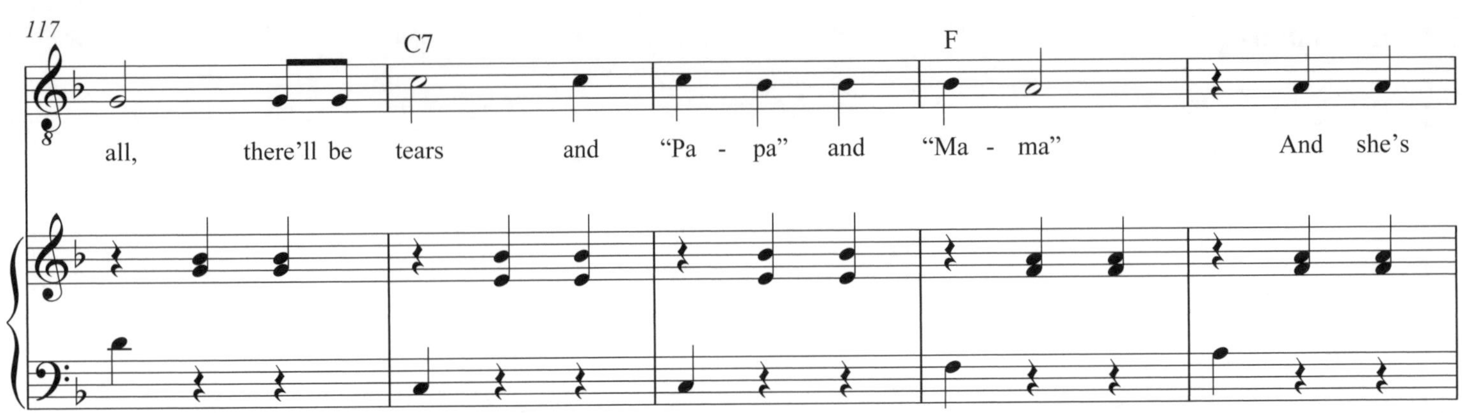
117
C7
F
all, there'll be tears and "Pa - pa" and "Ma - ma" And she's

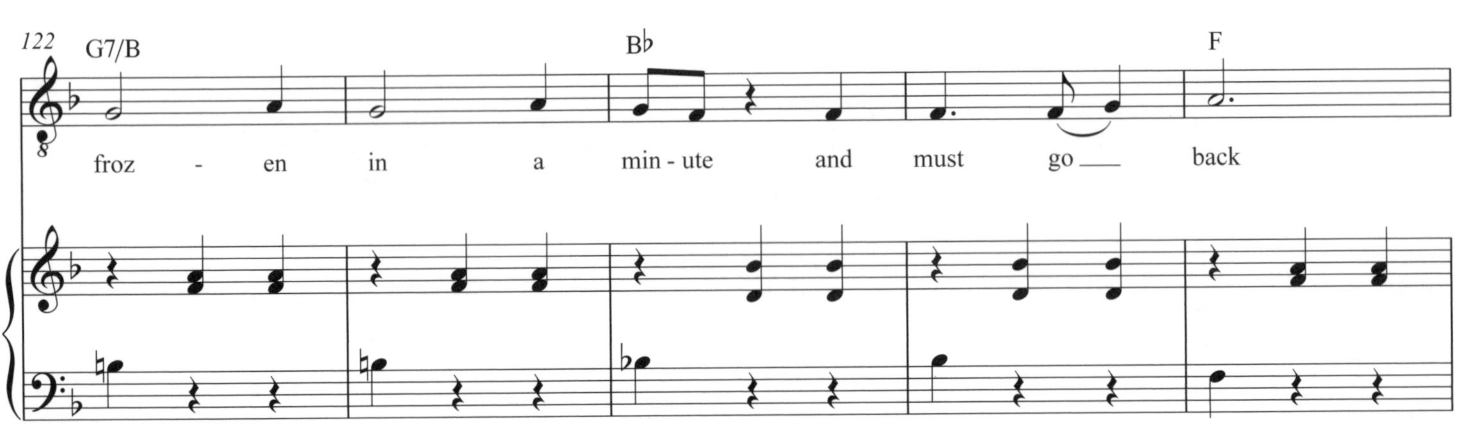
122
G7/B
B♭
F
froz - en in a min - ute and must go back

127
A7
But you wrap the fur cloak 'round her And you

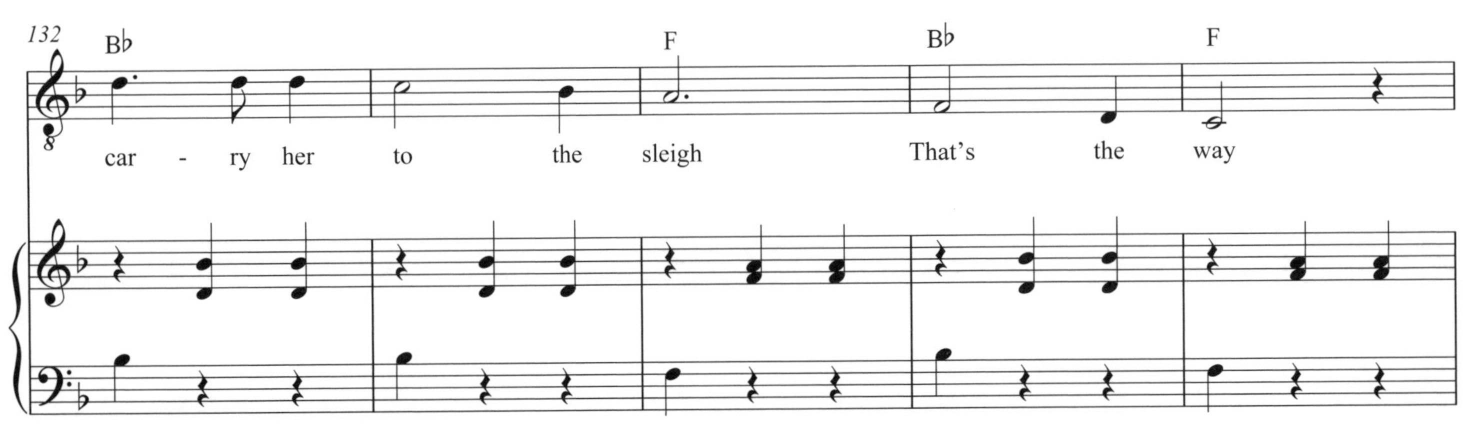
132
B♭
F
B♭
F
car - ry her to the sleigh That's the way

137
B♭
F
B♭
F
B♭
That's the way
CHORUS: mf
That's the way That's the
CHORUS: mf
That's the way That's the
142
F
♩ = 169
BALAGA: Let's get outta here!
way
way
[Horse hooves]
146
Bm
BALAGA: ff
And the troi - ka tore
f

150

down Ni - kit - ski Bou - le - vard

ALL: *ff*

Hey Ba - la - ga Ho Ba - la - ga

ALL: *ff*

Hey Ba - la - ga Ho Ba - la - ga

153

Hey hey ho __ Ba - la - ga Hey hey __ Ba - la - ga The fa - mous troi - ka driv - er

Hey hey ho __ Ba - la - ga Hey hey __ Ba - la - ga The fa - mous troi - ka driv - er

156

Hey Ba - la - ga Ho Ba - la - ga Hey hey hey __ Ba - la - ga Hey hey __ Ba - la - ga

Hey Ba - la - ga Ho Ba - la - ga Hey hey hey __ Ba - la - ga Hey hey __ Ba - la - ga

159
Cm
DOLOKHOV: f
When they reached the
The fa-mous troi - ka driv - er
The fa-mous troi - ka driv - er
162
Fm
Cm
gate Do - lo - khov whist-led
The
165
Fm
whist - le was an - swered, and a maid - ser - vant ran out

168
MAIDSERVANT: f
E
Come in through the courtyard or you'll be seen;
171
E7
she'll come out di - rect - ly
A
DOLOKHOV:
G
Do - lo-khov stayed by the
174
F♯7
gate
An - a - tole fol - lowed the
Bm
Em6
maid in - to the
177
Bm
Em6
court - yard Turned the
Bm
Em6
cor - ner, ran up to the
Fdim7
porch
ff

180
MARYA D.: ff
You will not en - ter my house, scoun - drel!
DOLOKHOV:
183
ff
An - a - tole, come back! Be - trayed! Be - trayed!
Am♯11
fff
186
Be - trayed, An - a - tole! Be - trayed! Come back! Be - trayed
189
An - a - tole! Be - trayed! Be - trayed!

PIERRE & ANDREY

Music and Lyrics by
DAVE MALLOY
Based on *War and Peace* by Leo Tolstoy

14
A7 Dm F+ A7/C♯ A7
ANDREY:
rit.
No, I am well There's a war going on For-
mp
mf
rit.
A tempo
18
Gm/A Dm/A A7 C♯dim7/A
give me for troub-ling you, I've re-ceived a re-fu-sal from Count-ess Ros-to-va And have heard re-ports of your
mp
20
D7/A Gm/A A7
molto rit.
PIERRE:
broth-er-in-law hav-ing sought her hand Or some-thing of that kind Is this true? Some-thing of that
molto rit.
23
Dm F B♭ F
a tempo
ANDREY:
kind Here are her let-ters Please give them to the
a tempo

27
C♯dim7
PIERRE:
Gm
ANDREY:
Dm
F/C
Count - ess Na - tash - a is ill She has been at death's door I much re - gret her
31
B♭
PIERRE:
Dm
F/C
B♭
B♭m
ill - ness And he smiled like his fa - ther Cold - ly, ma -
35
C♯dim7
C7
ANDREY:
Fm
Fm
PIERRE:
f
A♭/E♭
lic - ous - ly Well, it does - n't mat - ter. You told_ me once A
38
D♭
G♭
D♭
Fm
ANDREY:
f
A♭/E♭
D♭
A♭
mp
fall - en wom-an should be for - giv - en But I did - n't say that I could for - give I

41
C7
A tempo
Fm/C
C7
can't Yes, ask her hand a-gain Be mag-nan-i-mous, and so on Yes, that would be ver-y
mf
mp
44
D♭
rit.
D♭m
a tempo
A♭
no - ble But I can't be that man If you
rit.
p a tempo
47
B♭m
C7
Fm
wish to be my friend Nev-er speak of that a-gain Well, good-bye
50

PIERRE & NATASHA

Music and Lyrics by
DAVE MALLOY
Based on *War and Peace* by Leo Tolstoy

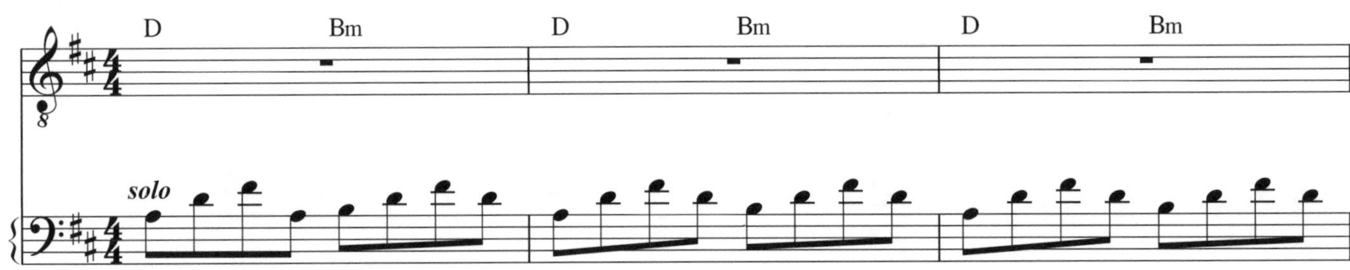

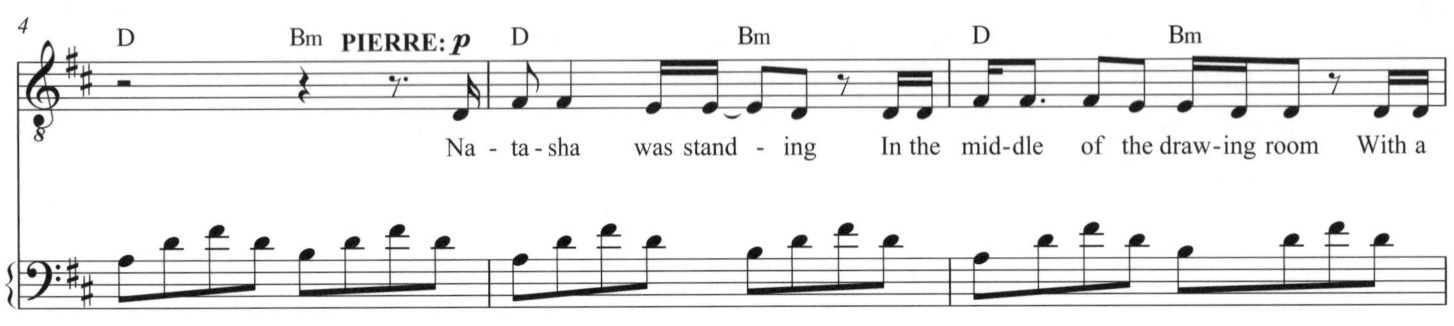

13
G
F♯7
G
stopped Breath-ing heav-i-ly Her thin arms hang-ing

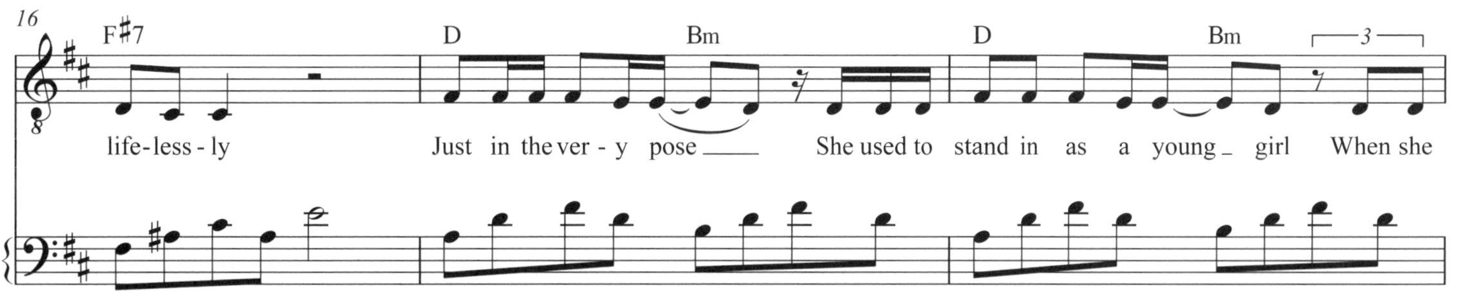
16
F♯7
D
Bm
D
Bm
3
life-less-ly Just in the ver-y pose She used to stand in as a young girl When she

19
D
Bm
D
Bm
D
Bm
went to the mid-dle of the ball-room to sing But the look on her face was quite

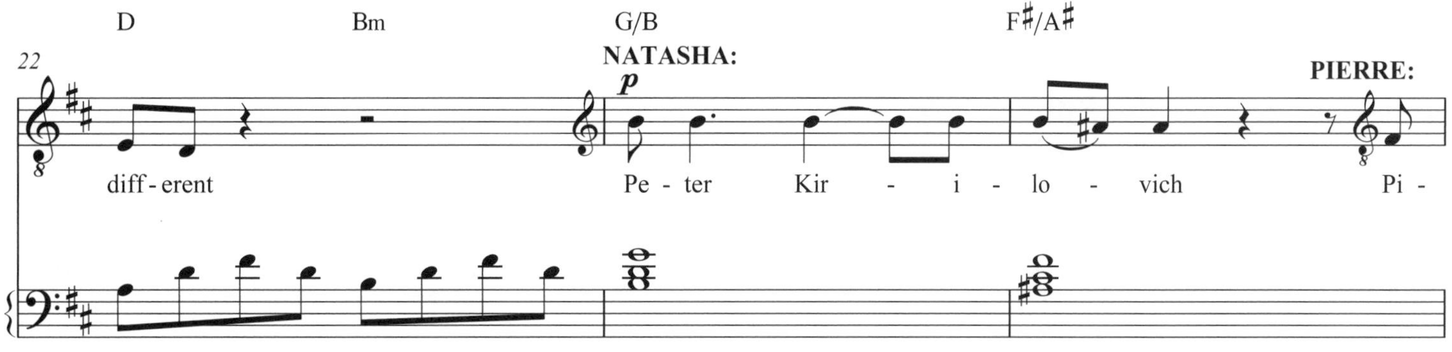
D
Bm
G/B
F♯/A♯
NATASHA:
PIERRE:
22
p
diff-erent Pe-ter Kir-i-lo-vich Pi-

25
Bm
D7
NATASHA:
D
Bm
erre Prince Bol-kon-sky was your friend

28
D
Bm
D
Bm
D
Bm
PIERRE:
He is your friend He once told me that I should turn to you Pi - erre

31
D
Bm
D
Bm
D
Bm
sniffed as he looked at her, but he did-n't speak 'Til then he had re-proached her, and

34
D
Bm
G
F#7
tried to des-pise her But now he felt such pit-y for her That there was no

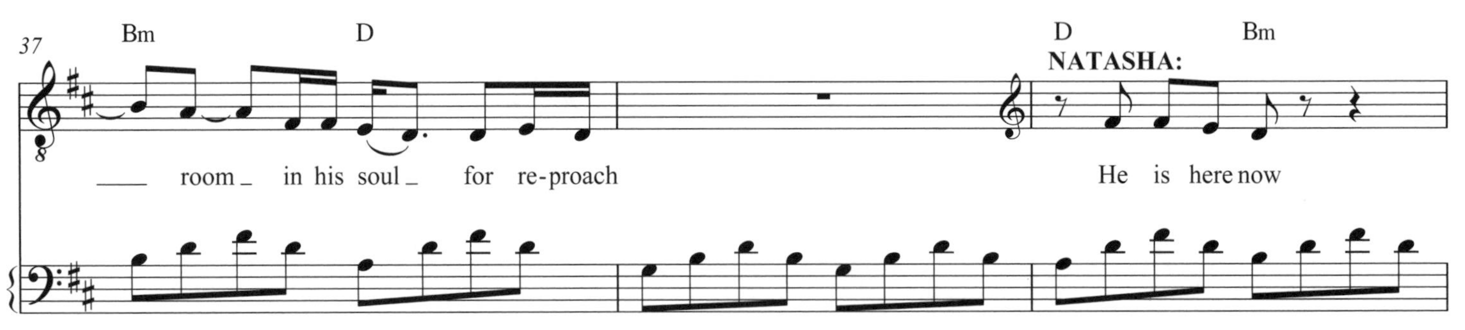
37
Bm
D
D
Bm
NATASHA:
room in his soul for re-proach He is here now

40
D
Bm
D
Bm
D
Bm
PIERRE:
Tell him to tell him to for-give me Yes, I will tell

43
D
Bm
3
D
Bm
NATASHA:
G
him to for-give you But, he gave me your let - ters No, I know that all is

46
F♯7
Bm
D
G
o - ver I know that it nev - er can be But

49
Bm
F♯/A♯
Bm
still I'm tor-ment - ed by the wrongs I've done him Tell him that I beg him to for-give

D
B♭+
rit.
3
52
PIERRE:
for-give For-give me for ev - ery-thing Yes, I will

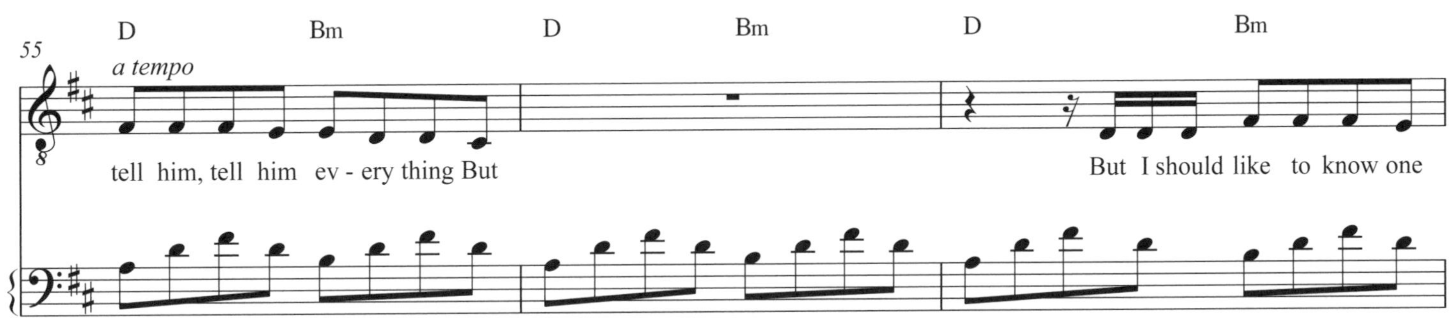
55
D
Bm
D
Bm
D
Bm
a tempo
tell him, tell him ev - ery thing But But I should like to know one

58
D Bm G F♯7
thing Did you love Did you love that bad
61
Bm D Gmaj7 D Bm
NATASHA:
rit.
a tempo
man? Don't call him bad But I don't
64
D Bm D Bm D Bm
know, I don't know at all
67
D Bm D Bm D Bm
PIERRE:
She be - gan to cry And a great - er sense of pit - y,
l.h.
70
D Bm D Bm D Bm
ten - der - ness, and love o - ver - flowed Pi - erre's heart He felt the

73
D Bm D Bm D Bm
3 3 3
tears be - gin to trick - le un - der - neath his spec - ta - cles And he hoped that no one would
76
D Bm G F♯7
3 3 3
see We won't speak of it a - ny - more We won't
79
Bm D G D Bm
speak of it, my dear But one thing I beg of you, con -
82
D Bm D Bm D Bm
3 3
sid - er me your friend And if you ev - er need help, or simp - ly to o - pen your heart to some - one Not
85
D Bm D Bm G
now, but when your mind is clear Think of me

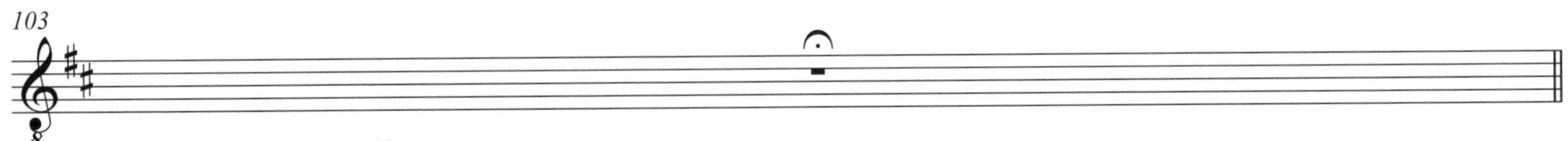

If I were not myself,
but the brightest, handsomest, best man on earth,
and if I were free,
I would get down on my knees this minute
and ask you for your hand and for your love.

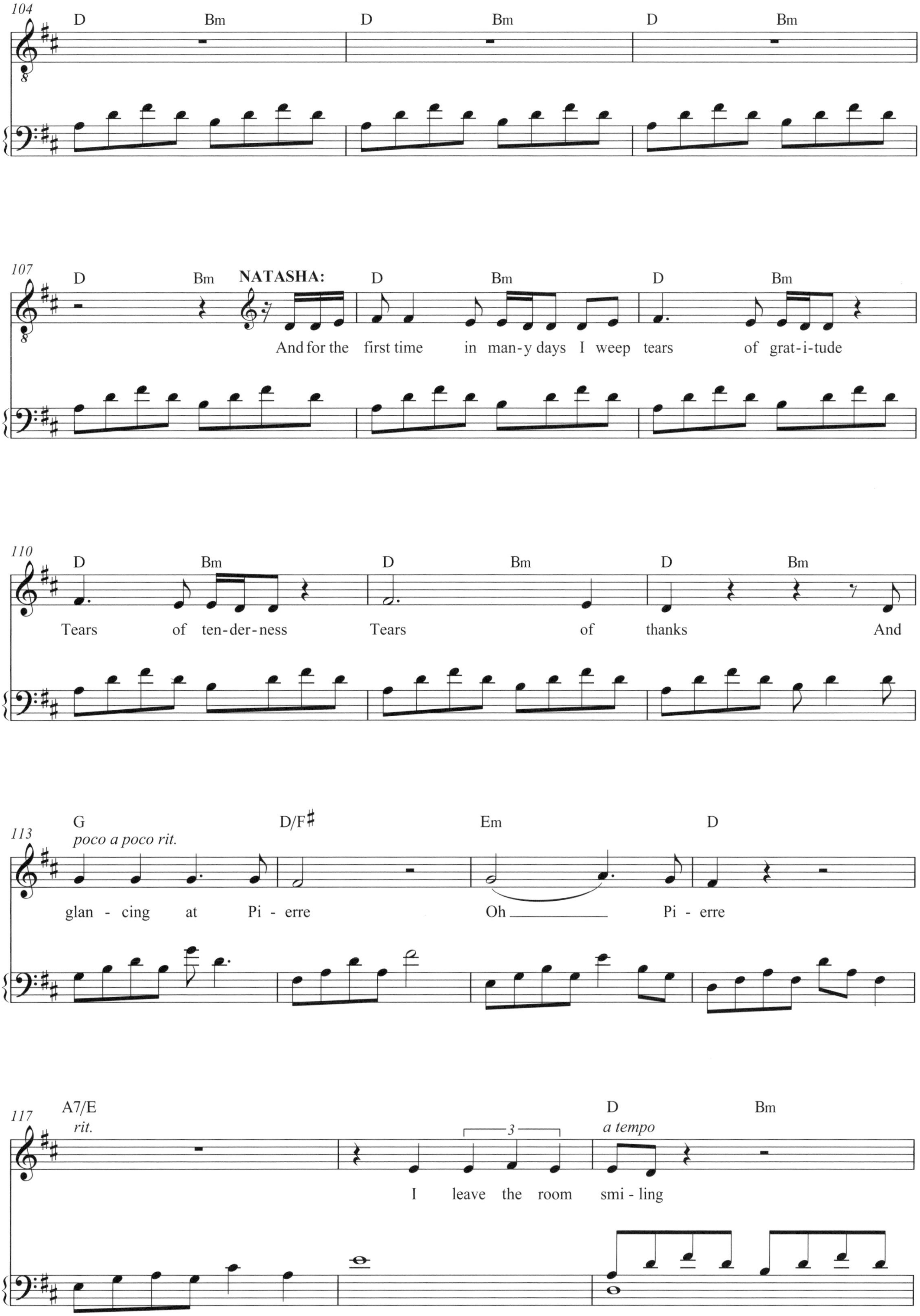

104
D Bm D Bm D Bm

107
D Bm **NATASHA:** D Bm D Bm
And for the first time in man-y days I weep tears of grat-i-tude

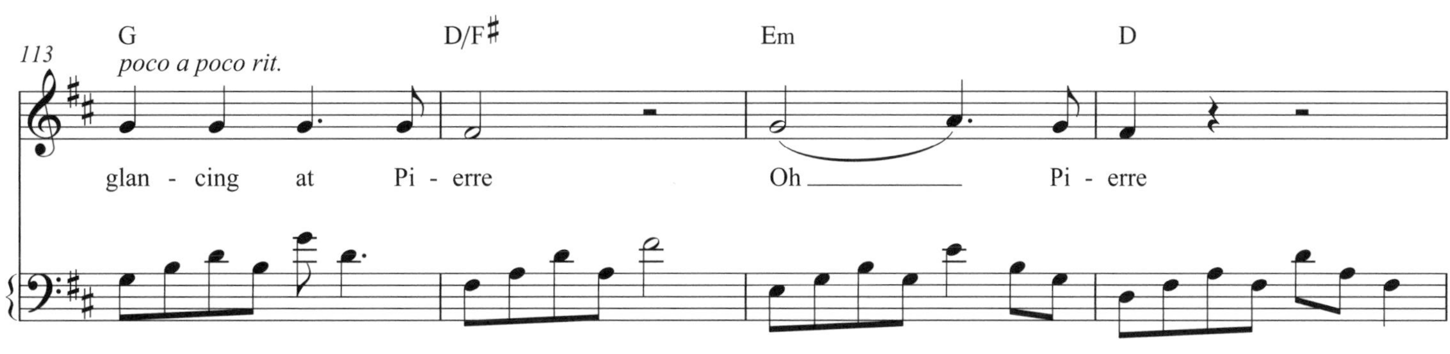

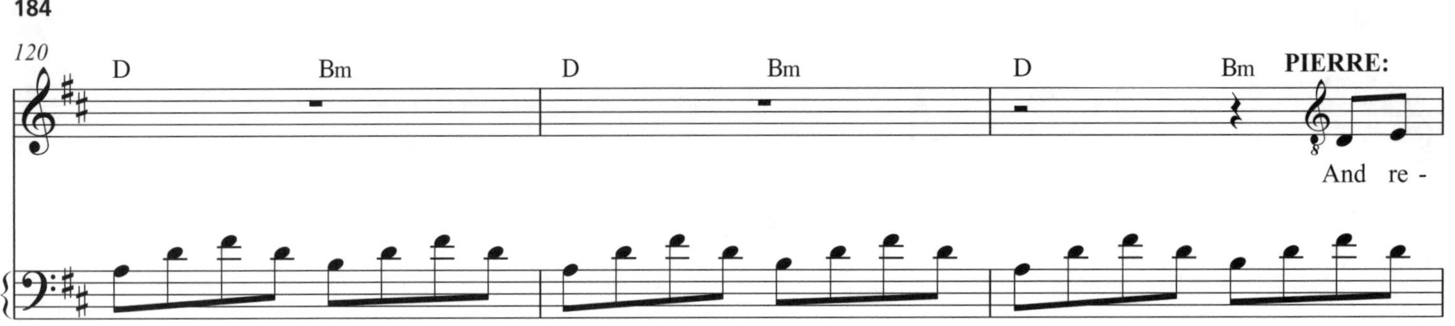
120
D
Bm
D
Bm
D
Bm
PIERRE:
And re -

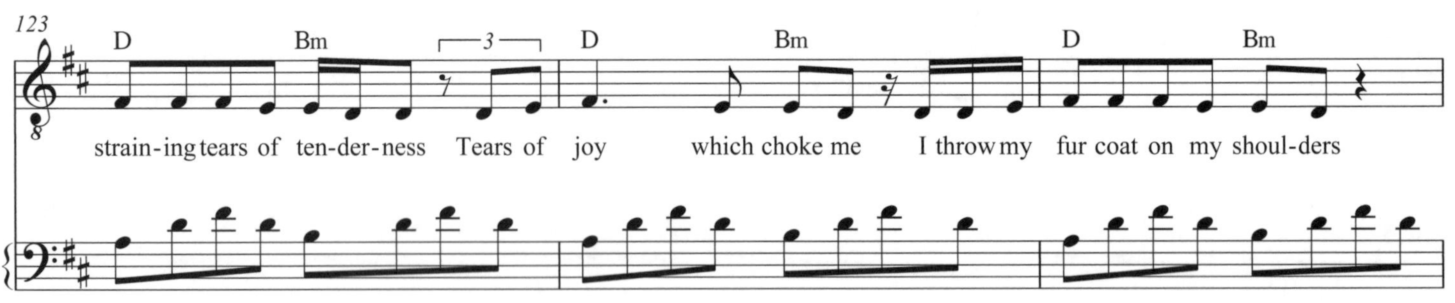
123
D
Bm
3
D
Bm
D
Bm
strain-ing tears of ten-der-ness Tears of joy which choke me I throw my fur coat on my shoul-ders

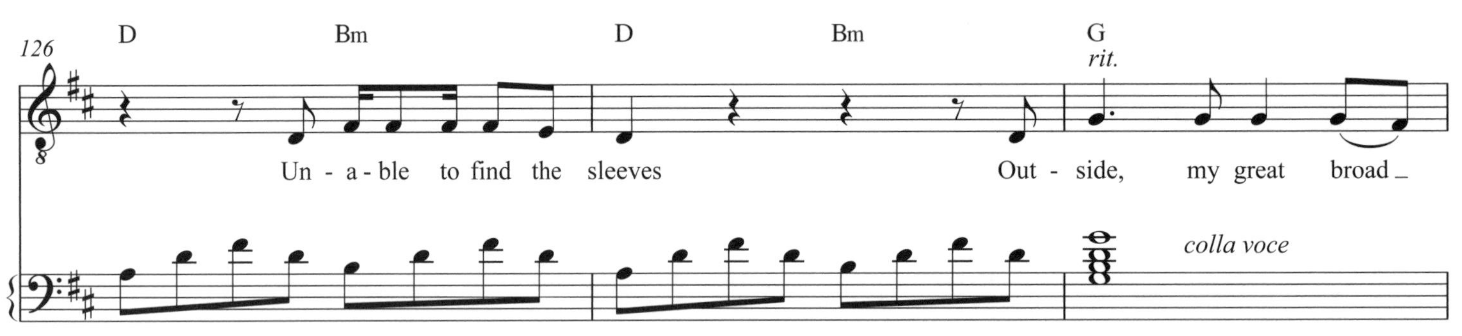
126
D
Bm
D
Bm
G
rit.
Un - a - ble to find the sleeves Out - side, my great broad
colla voce

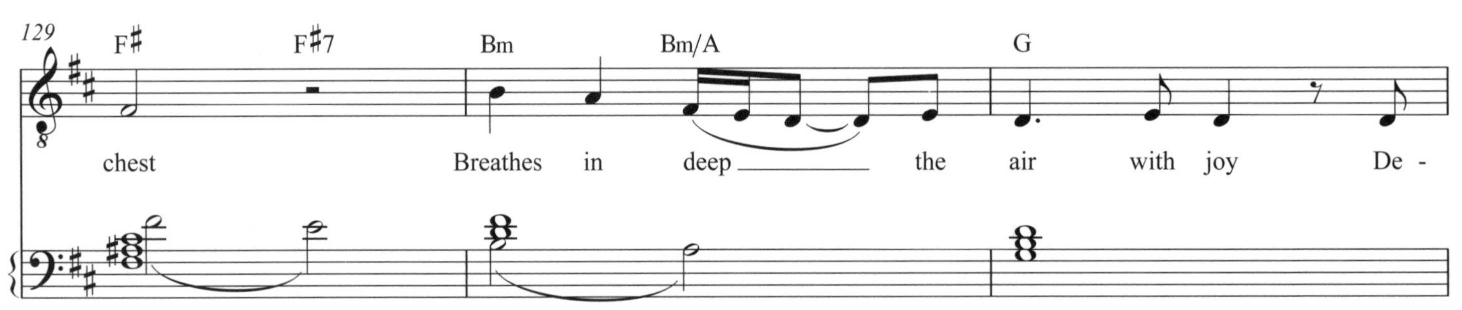
129
F♯
F♯7
Bm
Bm/A
G
chest Breathes in deep the air with joy De -

132
Em
A7
3
D
spite the ten de-grees of frost And I get in - to my sleigh

THE GREAT COMET OF 1812

Music and Lyrics by
DAVE MALLOY
Based on *War and Peace* by Leo Tolstoy

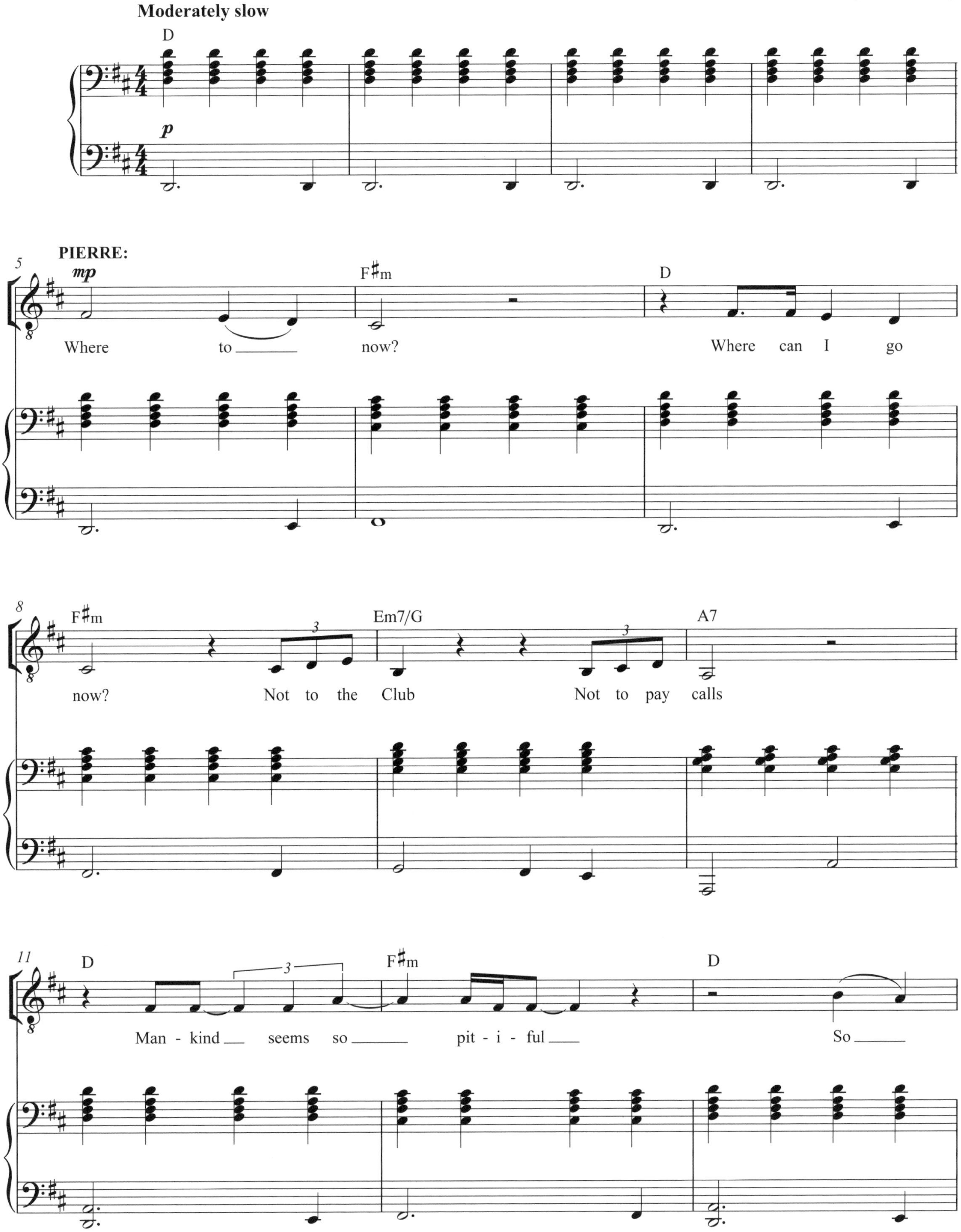

Moderately slow

D

p

5 **PIERRE:**

mp

F♯m D

Where to ___ now? Where can I go

8 F♯m Em7/G A7

now? Not to the Club Not to pay calls

11
D
F♯m
D
3
Man - kind ___ seems so ___ pit - i - ful ___
So ___

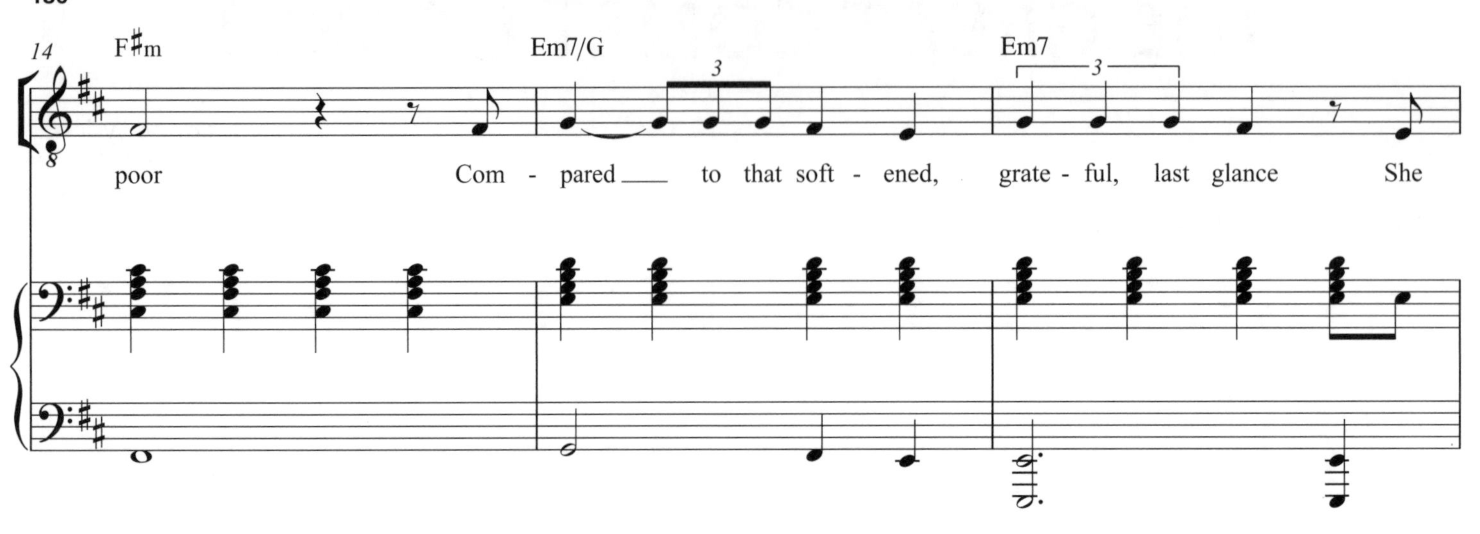
14
F♯m
Em7/G
Em7
3
poor Com - pared to that soft - ened, grate - ful, last glance She

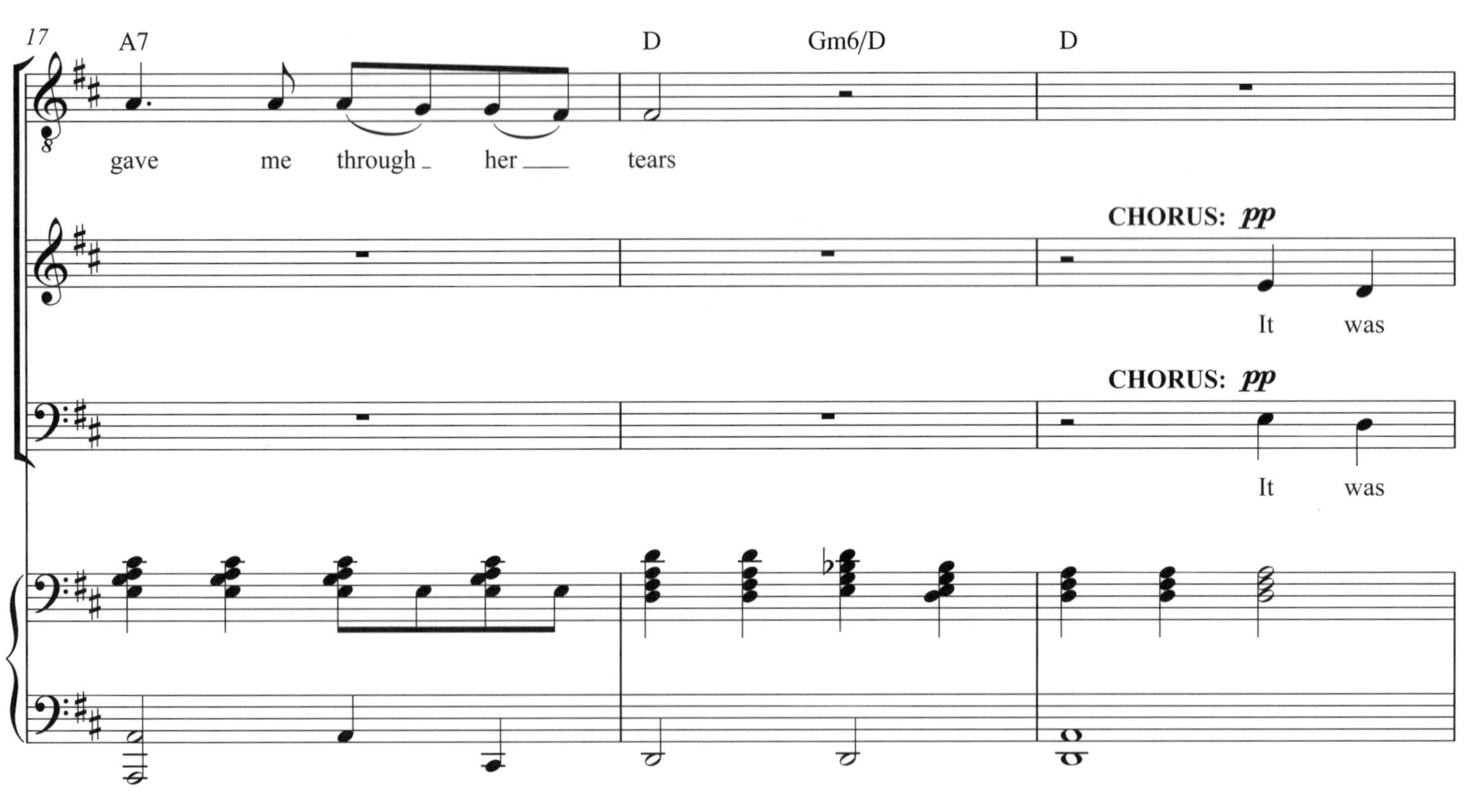
17
A7
D
Gm6/D
D
gave me through her tears
CHORUS: pp
It was
CHORUS: pp
It was

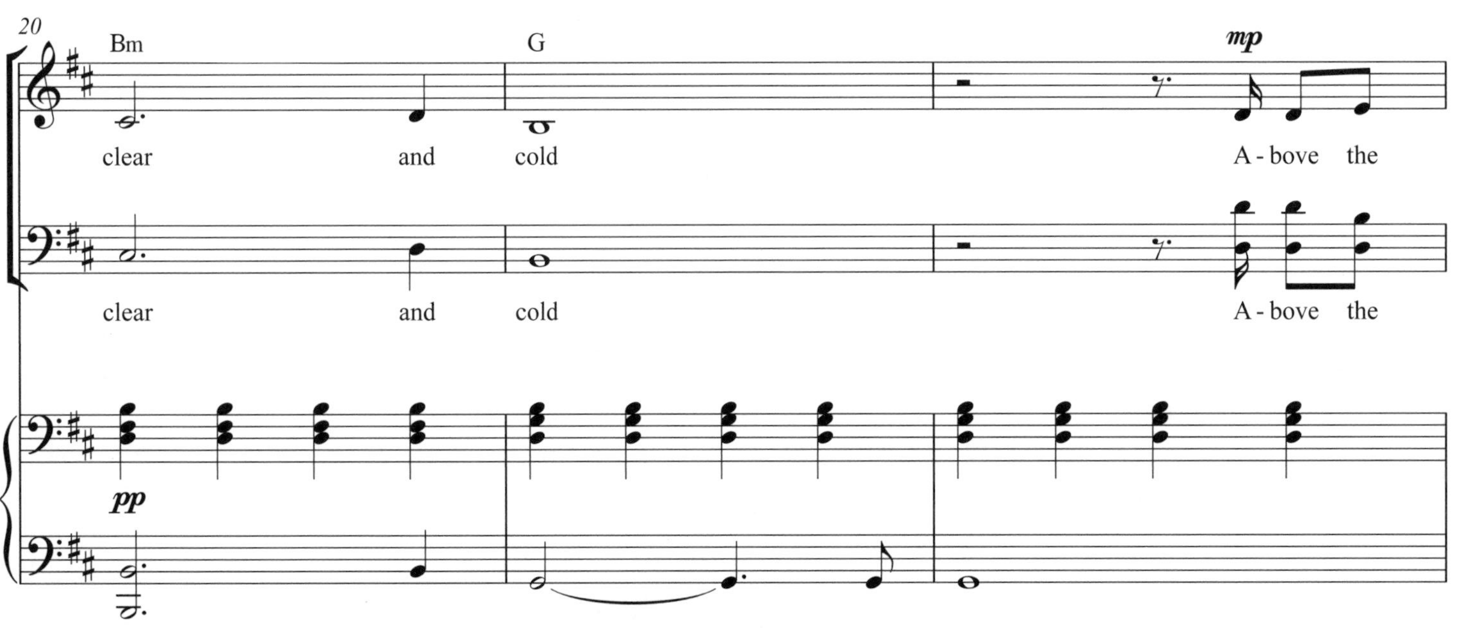
20
Bm
G
mp
clear and cold A - bove the
clear and cold A - bove the
pp

23
Em9
Gmaj7
A7
dir - ty streets A-bove the black roofs Stretched the dark star - ry
mp

26
F♯7
PIERRE:
Bm
Bm/A
This vast firm - a - ment O - pen to my
sky

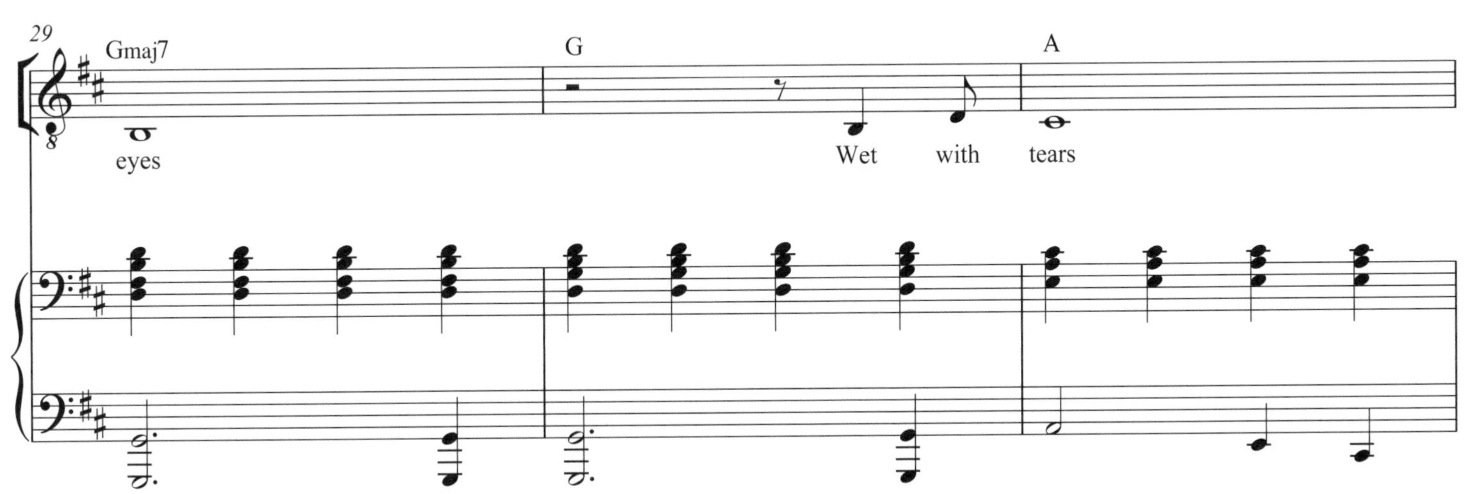
29
Gmaj7
G
A
eyes
Wet with tears

32

A7 | D |

CHORUS: *p*

F♯m

And there in the mid - dle A - bove

CHORUS: *p*

mf

35

D | F♯m | Em7/G

mf

Pre - chis - ten - sky Boul - e - vard ___ Sur - round - ed and

mf

38

B7/F♯ | Em | G♯dim7

ff

sprink - led on all sides by stars Shines The Great ___

41
F♯m/A
G
F♯7
G
Com - et of Eight - een Twelve The Brill - iant Com - et of Eigh - teen

44
D
PIERRE: mf
D+
3
D6
The com - et said to por - tend Un - told
Twelve
mp

47
D+
3
D
Gm6
hor - rors And the end of the world But for me The com-et brings no
mf

50
D/F♯
Em7
D
D7
f
G
F♯7
3
fear No, I gaze joy-ful-ly And this bright star Hav-ing
f
53
Bm
D7
G
D/F♯
Em7
D
3
traced its pa-rab-o-la With in-ex-press-a-ble speed Through im-meas-ura-ble space Seems
mf
56
Gm
C7
D
Gm6/D
D
rit.
a tempo
sud-den-ly To have stopped Like an ar-row pierc-ing the earth
rit.
p
a tempo
58
Em7
A7
mf
Stopped for me It

61

D F♯m D F♯m

seems to me That this com - et Feels me

CHORUS:

mf

Oo ______ Oo ______

CHORUS:

mf

mf

65

Em/G B7/F♯ Em

Feels my soft - ened and up - lift - ed soul

Oo ______

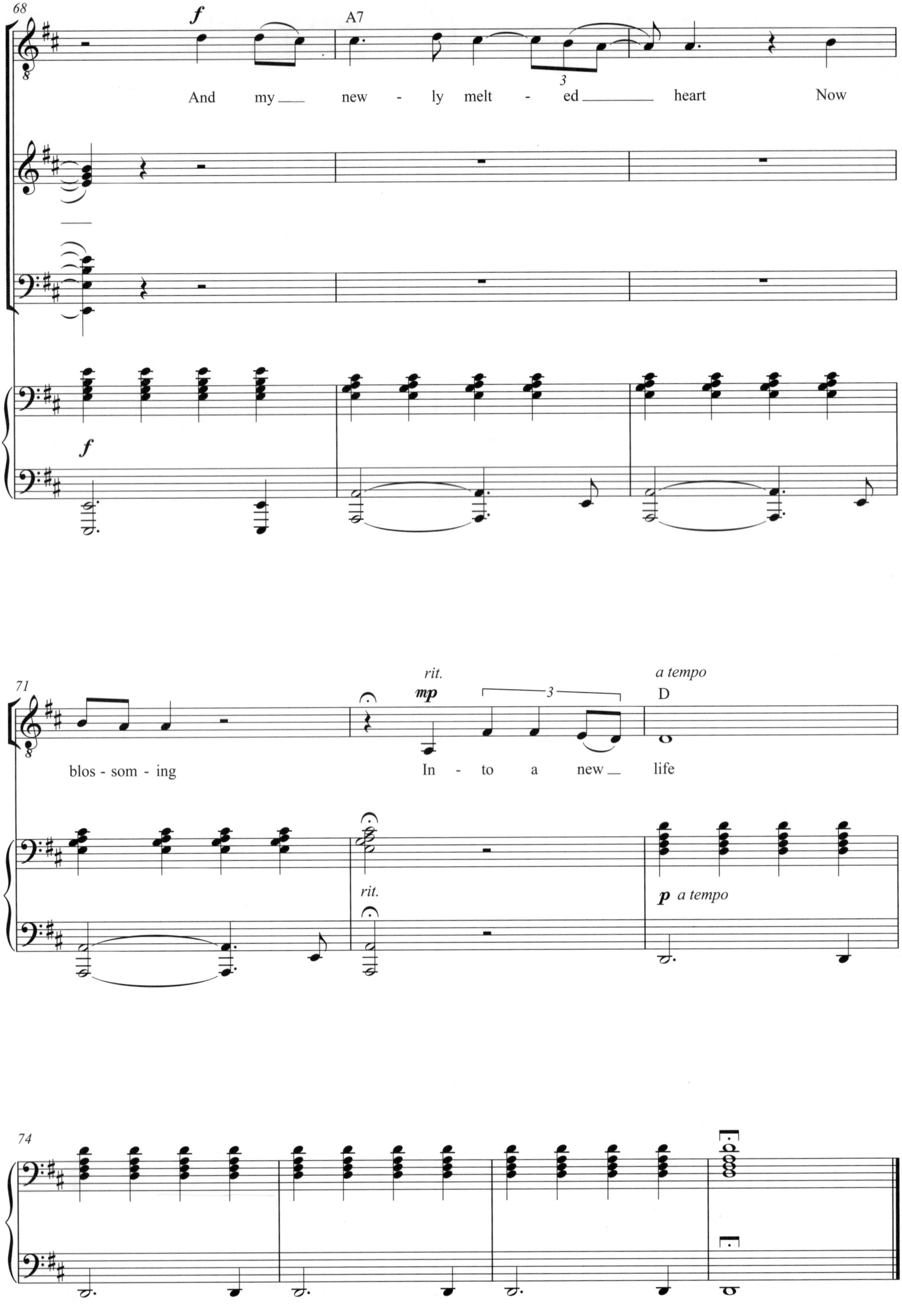

68

f A7

And my new - ly melt - ed heart Now

f